WE WERE SOLDIERS TOO

Book One
Serving as a Reagan Soldier
During the Cold War

Bob Kern

www.weweresoldierstoo.com

Edited by Brian Hawkins

We Were Soldiers Too/ Bob Kern. – 2nd edition.

Dedicated to my beloved mother, the person I respect most in this world. You successfully raised five kids alone and always set an example for us to follow. I thank God every day for allowing me to be your son.

And to my amazing wife, who somehow manages to put up with me, day after day, year after year. You are the perfect grandmother, mother, and most importantly, wife.

Special thanks to Randall Kranepuhl, Troy E Dickerson, and Samuel R Young

Table of Contents

Forward

September 11, 2001 started like every other morning. I climbed into my car and turned the radio on to listen to *The Bob and Tom Show*. To my surprise, I immediately noticed the usual banter and raunchy jokes were absent, replaced by somber commentary from the hosts. I quickly realized this wasn't one of their absurd skits. I sat there in my drive way in total disbelief as they went over details of a plane flying into one of the World Trade Center towers. Like everyone that morning, I was in complete shock over this news.

Driving to work, I continued to listen to the details of the first crash when reports of another plane flying into the second tower started coming in. My shock quickly turned to anger. This was no accident but a deliberate attack by some terrorist group. The boldness to attack the United States of America was beyond belief. Thoughts of the attack on Pearl Harbor, an attack which drew us into World War II, came to mind. Where would this lead us? There was no doubt we would make those behind this attack pay.

When I arrived at work, I rushed inside to supplement this radio news with my computer, anxious for more information. I watched replays of the planes hitting the towers while listening to live coverage on the radio. Reports started coming in of another plane crashing into the Pentagon. It was pure chaos as everyone scrambled to keep up with the madness of that morning. News of a hijacked fourth plane that would later crash in a field in Pennsylvania began coming in.

Then the most horrific event imaginable happened. First one Twin Tower collapsed, and shortly after, the second one came down. *Oh my God!* I thought. All those people inside, including the first responders who went in to help people get out were gone.

In the days that followed, the country cried together for the victims and their families while we watched the rescue workers relentlessly search through the rubble for survivors. Then we got angry. As we heard each new detail of this deliberate attack, we wanted those responsible to pay for this. We put our political differences aside and stood as one nation for the first time in my lifetime. We quietly cheered when President Bush announced that we were going after the terrorists behind this act and any country that supported and harbored these lunatics.

Something else happened that day, something the terrorists never considered when they were planning this attack. Patriotism. This tragedy reminded us that we were the greatest country in the world and no terrorist act was going to change this. American flags found their way out of Independence Day storage boxes. People rummaged through attics and sheds for old flags that hadn't flown in years. The Stars and Stripes appeared in front yards and windows across the country. Everywhere I looked, I saw Old Glory. Hearing the national anthem caused everyone to sing as loud as they could, voices rising as one, sharing in this newfound national pride. I found myself holding back tears and fighting the urge to cry like a baby every time I heard it. Still do.

I was never more proud of my service than during the time immediately following 9/11. I am sure all veterans shared this pride. Vets physically fit and young enough, reenlisted, while others had circumstances that prevented it. Disabled veterans would've been the first in line had they been fit enough to reenlist. All veterans lived vicariously through our brothers in arms as they contributed to this cause. We mourned at each casualty but knew the soldiers who gave their lives in this fight against terrorism died with valor. When you enlist, you do so with the knowledge that you could go to war and lose your life. That's why you join the military. Whether you serve during peacetime or declared war, you join because you are willing to sacrifice your life for your country.

At some point during the next year, something unexpected happened to me. I began getting thanks for my service from people when they learned I was a veteran. I realized they thought I had served during this war and were thanking me for it. I felt ashamed that I hadn't been in combat and felt guilty accepting thanks from people who had made this assumption. For a while, I would thank them, then explain I was a Reagan soldier, serving during his eight years as president, and never went to war.

The first Veterans Day after 9/11 my church honored veterans the day before. My preacher asked the veterans in the church to stand up but I remained seated because of the shame I felt. At my wife and granddaughters urging, I finally did stand while the congregation clapped and cheered for us. I felt undeserving of their applause. I knew they were making the same assumption that I had fought in the war and I felt like I was deceiving them all. This guilt was overwhelming and added to the shame I feel as a peacetime veteran.

I started dreading Veterans Day because I knew I had to go to my grandchildren's schools for their Veterans Day programs. I had three different schools to visit and knew I would be asked to stand up at two and go on stage with other veterans for the third. The guilt I felt for this would eat me up each year.

Over time, I realized my service was nothing to feel ashamed of. I served during a critical period of the Cold War and the nuclear arms race. Those who served during this era contributed to preventing a nuclear war. Our training and preparations served as a deterrent to the Soviets, keeping them in check until their eventual implosion and the fall of the Berlin Wall.

I volunteered and would have gone to war if the nation required it. Thankfully, for the sake of our country, I never had to. A confrontation would have led to nuclear war. Both sides had nuclear weapons and would have used them. Nobody would have won a nuclear war.

I am certain there are many veterans just like me. To be a veteran who never went to war can be a heavy burden. This led me to realize there are veterans who served in support roles during this war on terrorism but never in combat. There are soldiers who served in reserve and support units that never deployed overseas but were prepared to if needed. I feel certain these veterans deal with the same mixed emotions I do when being thanked for my service. No veteran should ever be ashamed for serving their country.

So I decided to write this book. I wanted to share what it was like to serve during the Cold War era. I thought my story might somehow make people recognize the contributions of all veterans is important no matter when or where they served. There should be no distinguishing whether veterans served in combat or not. Especially when we have an all-voluntary military. If people are willing to serve, and if necessary die for their country, the circumstances under which they served is irrelevant. And most importantly, veterans should always be proud for serving their country.

I do not want to diminish those who fought during this war on terrorism. I admire them just as I admired those I served with whom had fought in the Vietnam War.

This book is my story. I wanted to share what it was like serving in the Army during this critical time in history.

Chapter 1
Basic Training

I decided to enlist in the army one month after my seventeenth birthday. After finishing my sophomore year at Yorktown High School in 1979, I moved to Alexandria, Indiana. When I enrolled in school, I learned I had accumulated enough credits to graduate a year early if I took one extra course at night school. I was eager to finish high school so I jumped at this opportunity.

I was blessed to have an amazing mom. She raised five kids on her own and never complained. We didn't have much money and we didn't need it. We ate lots of peanut butter and bologna sandwiches, and her fried chicken every Sunday was a feast fit for kings. But college was expensive and I knew we couldn't afford for me to go. She would have found a way to pay for it, but I knew how difficult this would have been. I was graduating a year early and had never submitted any college applications. I announced that I was going to take a year off before college, but the truth was I hadn't given much thought to what I was going to do after high school. I was content with my job pumping gas, and the freedoms I was enjoying my final year of high school. I was anxious for school to end so I could go full-time at work and have more money and more freedom. My future concerns never went beyond the upcoming weekend. My closest friend in high school was Paul Copley who was five years older than I was. We were so much alike that we never noticed the age difference. When school started, Paul had moved into his own home just outside Yorktown's city limit. His house was only ten minutes from Alexandria and by the end of the school year I was spending every weekend there. Paul had a younger brother named Don who had joined the Army right after I had moved to Alexandria. Don graduated from basic training in April of 1980 and came home for leave before heading off to Fort Leonard Wood, Missouri for his Military Occupation Specialty (MOS) training.

Don was very excited about completing basic training and talked to me a lot about his experiences. Listening to his stories got me interested in the army and I decided I wanted to join. Like any teenager, I was clueless about what this commitment meant but I was so excited about this decision that I didn't care about the particulars anyway.

The day I decided to enlist was the day of my senior prom. I raced home to change into my dashing, light blue tuxedo and break the news to my mother. As expected, she cried and told me how proud she was of me but she never once questioned my decision. Just another reminder of why I am proud to be her son.

I was clueless when I saw my recruiter with no idea what to expect. Recruiters focused on filling quotas instead of assigning kids to jobs they wanted or qualified for. They would flat-out lie to get whatever position they needed to fill then.

One trick they used worked in my favor, allowing me to enter basic training as an E-2 private. This paid more and gave me a jump on the promotion ladder. This was done using a referral program the army offered to recruits who referred two friends who also enlisted. Some recruiters, like mine, cheated and used this program to push kids towards the spots they needed to fill. They credited me with the names of recruits they had already signed to give me the referrals I needed for this promotion. A great carrot to guide trusting teenagers, like myself, to whatever jobs the recruiters wanted.

I was one of the more naïve ones when I enlisted. I hoped to see the world and the only thing I knew for sure was I wanted to go to Germany. I took the placement test that was supposed to help put me in the job I was best qualified for. I am confident that my scores on this test played no part in the MOS they signed me up for. The recruiter knew I wanted Germany and used this information to get me where he wanted. He made a big show of scanning my test and comparing it to other reports. He informed me that I was in luck, he had one slot open in Germany that I qualified for. The position was Heavy Anti-Armor Crewman, an MOS known by the army as 11HE9.

What an awesome title! I thought. Heavy Anti-Armor Crewman. So, I signed on the dotted line swelling with excitement and pride. I went home and bragged to everyone that would listen, telling them of my big title. That following weekend Don called to find out how my enlistment went. I told him my new fancy title. He was unfamiliar with it so he asked me what my MOS was. When I said it was 11HE9, he laughed and informed me that I was a grunt. My heart sank and I thought I was going to be sick. A grunt. I had no idea what a grunt was but the word grunt filled me with dread. Anything referred to as a grunt couldn't be good.

As soon as I graduated from high school, I was ready to spread my wings so I moved in with Paul. I was soon sent to Indianapolis where I got my physical and had my initial swearing-in ceremony. I was scheduled to attend basic training in November and sent home. I went back to Paul's house and spent the next six months enjoying life to its fullest doing what you would expect two young guys to do. I enjoyed this reprieve a bit too much, surviving on a diet of fast-food. I gained more than thirty pounds that summer.

Eventually, all good must end and as summer turned to fall, the time arrived for me to leave. My mom drove me to Indianapolis where I reported for duty. I went through the final stages of enlisting and sworn in again to reaffirm my commitment to enlist for four years. The next morning, I was put on a bus and sent to Fort Jackson, South Carolina to process into the army before being sent to Fort Benning for basic training.

I arrived at Fort Jackson to a friendly welcome. The barracks and surrounding buildings looked new and the mess hall looked like a country club cafeteria. I unpacked before reporting to the front of the barracks. I spent the next hour learning how to fall into various formations and the basics of marching. The instructor was very polite and patient as he marched us around the parking lot. I decided that this wasn't going to be so bad after all.

The next morning after breakfast, I went to the quartermaster. It seemed like they measured every part of my body before I issuing me uniforms. The fatigues were a funky shade of green I had never seen before called olive drab. I am certain this color played a part when coming up with the word "drab" in its name. Supposedly, this color provided the best camouflage in a wooded environment. I got four sets of "olive drab' fatigues and two sets of the Class A dress uniforms. Even my socks and t-shirts were olive drab. I issued everything I would need to wear, including skivvies. The one thing that should have been olive drab was white, go figure. I put my civilian clothes in a bag, olive drab of course, and I wouldn't see them again until I graduated basic training and arrived in Germany.

I continued learning the very basics of the military while getting shots, filling out records, making a will, and completing countless other forms of paperwork- including writing a letter home. I realize now this to make sure our mothers thought we were happy little soldiers. They showed me how to wear my new uniforms per military standards. They taught me how to set up my locker the proper way with rolled socks, t-shirts, and undies all lined up neatly, and uniforms hung and facing the same way with the sleeves tucked in. Everything had a place in the army and uniformity was the word of the day. They continued to work with me on marching and formations trying to get me prepared for the strict regimen I was about to face.

Thanksgiving, my first major holiday in the military and away from home, caused me to spend a little longer time at Fort Jackson than most soldiers did. The mess hall served a traditional Thanksgiving meal with all the trimmings and it tasted good. Yep, this wasn't going to be bad at all. Before I knew it, I found myself on a bus heading to Fort Benning.

Chapter 2
Arriving at Fort Benning

I arrived at basic training expecting to be welcomed in a manner like what I had just experienced at Fort Jackson. I couldn't have been more wrong. No sooner had the buses parked when the yelling began. Drill instructors entered each bus using extremely colorful language and barking orders for us to exit the bus and quickly form up outside. Wide-awake now - terror has this affect - I quickly exited the bus and fell into formation with the rest of the platoon. I was ordered to do push-ups until I could no longer push up no matter how hard I pushed. Just when I was certain that I was about to die, they allowed us to stop, ending the pain for the moment. We formed into platoon formation and marched to my assigned barracks.

In my training company, the platoons and barracks were divided by MOS. We were all infantry soldiers, or grunts, but I soon realized that there are different types of grunts. My platoon consisted of all the trainees for 11H heavy anti-armor weapons grunts. There was another platoon with all the 11C indirect fire grunts, and last two platoons of your basic 11B grunts. Expecting to be released from this abuse, instead, I was forced to do more push-ups. There I was, a scared out-of-shape teenager, lying on my belly trying to look like I was doing push-ups when I was praying to wake up from this nightmare. As I laid there with my arms shaking and weak, and my face flushed, I was certain my eyes were going to pop out of my head if I pushed any harder. This whole time I was being told I was the lowest form of life on earth, lower than worms. The berating continued relentlessly and they kept calling us a bunch of maggots, a name they seemed to like to call recruits because they would use it all the time. My stomach churned and terror filled every fiber of my body as I realized my life was now in the hands of these raging madmen called drill sergeants.

Exhausted, weak and terrified of saying or doing the wrong thing, I was finally allowed to enter my barracks, an old, two story building nothing like the apartment-type barracks I had just left. The first thing I saw when I entered the bathroom was the showers. Excuse me, the latrine. Calling it anything else, I quickly learned, resulted in more punishment and humiliation.

When I entered the latrine, the first thing I noticed was sinks and mirrors lining both walls. Immediately to the left was the shower room, a tiled room with wall-to-wall showers. But the biggest shock was the room to the right. Upon entering it, I didn't even notice the urinals lining the left wall. Nope, what caught my attention was the row of toilets, side-by-side with nothing dividing them. Nothing. I didn't even like using public restrooms so how was I supposed to do this?

Guys aren't like women who will chat it up with the woman in the next stall. When we go to the movies with a buddy, we always leave an empty seat between us. It's the same with public restrooms. We always make sure there is a urinal between us and we never talk to the guy next to us. No way! It's always eyes to the front, staring at the wall, then wash your hands and leave without a word said. I found my heart racing as I realized I would have to do my serious business with no privacy at all.

Past this was a large open room with a row of bunk beds down each side. Two adjacent lockers made a partition that separated each set of bunks. The room had a large rectangular outline painted on the center of the floor with a huge airborne insignia in the center. Upstairs had a couple of small rooms that the drill instructors slept in and another large bunk area just like downstairs. I was assigned a top bunk on the second floor.

After finding my bed, I began unpacking like I had been taught, clothes hung orderly and socks and t-shirts rolled and laid out uniformly in the drawers. Once completed, we were all summoned to the upstairs corner of the barracks where I met my drill instructors, including my senior instructor Sergeant First-Class Lee. He welcomed us and for a few minutes I got to experience my TV-like moment of basic. Sitting and standing around him, we all shared a little bit about ourselves and where we were from. This family moment passed soon enough and the door to hell was thrown wide open.

I was ordered back to my bunk area and told to fall in at attention along the line facing inward. Then, in a way only drill sergeants can, I was reminded of my lowly wormlike status. Terrified, I stood there and listened as my drill sergeant informed me that the center of the barracks was off limits. Since I wasn't airborne qualified, if I touched the area inside the lines with the logo I would be disrespecting the honor of those who were airborne qualified. In fact, I wasn't even worthy enough to touch the line that bordered this area. I didn't need to be told twice, so I never touched that line. I would skirt it sideways to get to and from my bunk the entire time I was there. I was finally ordered to bed but I didn't sleep much that first night.

Before I knew it, I awakened by a large clamor and shouting coming from downstairs. As the noise made its way up the stairs, I realized it was SFC Lee causing all the ruckus. He was banging two trash-can lids together like a lunatic and shouting orders to get up and form up along the line on the floor. I was immediately wide-awake and standing at my assigned spot on that line. I am sure I made quite the picture standing there along that stupid line in my underwear, eyes staring straight ahead as I prayed silently that I hadn't done something to draw attention to me. I was then released and given two minutes to dress and form up in front of the barracks for my first session of physical training.

Just when I didn't think it could get any worse, it did. SFC Lee held up orange fluorescent vests when he addressed the platoon. My heart sank when he told us these vests were for his fat boys and then he handed me one. The door to hell hadn't only opened; I had just been shoved through it. I was regretting every fast food meal I had enjoyed that past summer.

Those of us labeled fat boys were given these vests and told we were to be road guards for the entire duration of basic training. We were responsible for blocking traffic as the platoon marched or ran by intersections. There were four of us, two positioned in the front of the formation and two in the rear. The front two would run ahead to upcoming intersections and hold traffic for the platoon. The back two would run up and relieve them as the platoon arrived to the intersection and hold traffic until everyone had passed the intersection. I quickly realized this was his grand weight loss plan by making us run twice as much during PT with extra running when we were marching. I vowed to myself to get off the fat boy list as fast as possible.

I was so determined to lose weight quickly and remove myself from the fat boy list I practically starved myself the first month. Not the healthiest way to lose weight, but it worked and turned out to be quite profitable for me. At each meal, I sold my meat and dessert for a dollar each. I hated wearing that road-guard vest, not because it marked me as a fat boy, but for the pain it always brought. It's impossible to hide your struggles when you are outside the formation and wearing a bright, florescent orange vest. I couldn't fall out of formation to catch my breath or puke when I was responsible for stopping traffic as the platoon ran through each intersection. I lost weight fast and by Christmas SFC Lee was no longer referring to me as one of his fat boys. Nevertheless, I continued being a road guard for the rest of basic training, so I guess he hadn't completely forgotten. Consequently, I developed a high tolerance for pain during this time. I didn't want to do anything that drew the drill instructor's attention my way, so I shouldn't have been surprised that it worked.

It's no secret that basic training is supposed to be hard. The army doesn't need unfit people trying to protect the country. When I enlisted, I expected to be pushed to my physical limits but what I wasn't prepared for was the mental abuse I had to take. I had heard rumors of drill sergeants physically abusing recruits in the past. I have no idea of the truth of those rumors. I do know that when I was there in 1980 they would get in serious trouble for striking a recruit. I quickly found out that they didn't need to hit me to get my attention anyway. Fear and humiliation was a much more effective tool to strip away self-worth and turn trainees into followers.

Later in my career, I took a college management course that covered different management styles. One of these was the Theory X and Theory Y style of management. Theory X was the belief that people are lazy and need constant supervision to get something done. Theory Y is the belief that people are good and will always do their jobs without constant supervision. Neither of these styles work in the civilian world. I was taught the only time Theory X could work was in a combat environment where soldiers needed to respond to orders without question and with complete faith in the leader giving the order. A big part of basic training was to transform recruits into followers who wouldn't question their leaders.

My experience in basic training confirmed this. It was the responsibility of the drill sergeants to break me down mentally and make me so weak that I would blindly follow those in charge of me. They were good at making me feel worthless and incapable of making my own decisions. The abuses they put me through mentally to mold me into a soldier changed me forever, which of course, was the objective. Fear is a great motivator and I lived in a constant state of fear.

I was terrified of my drill sergeants and anyone else I encountered with rank. But the people who treated recruits the worst were the drill corporals. These were soldiers who had only recently completed basic training and had been given temporary promotions to corporal. The logic for this was probably that these guys could better communicate with trainees. They had just gone through a process designed to make them soldiers who would blindly follow orders. As a reward for finishing at the top of the class, they found themselves working beside the drill sergeants they had just come to worship. They were completely unprepared for these roles and had no idea what being a good leader meant or looked like. Taking soldiers fresh out of basic training and placing them in a leadership positions over vulnerable recruits is not a very smart thing to do. This boneheaded policy quite often led to power trips with these guys. In many cases, they ridiculed recruits for their own twisted pleasure. Some of the things they did was excessive and only served their bloated egos at the expense of the recruits' dignity.

The humiliation I was subjected to did what it was supposed to. I quickly learned my place at the bottom of the pecking order and how to be good little soldier. This didn't change the abuse because it was a form of brain washing and the pressure had to remain to ensure I never forgot that soldiers take orders and follow them, no questions asked.

Sleep deprivation was another tool used to change me into a soldier. A tired brain made me react to commands unquestioningly, making the mental abuse I went through more effective. My body was learning through repetition while my mind was kept sluggish. I was being turned into a follower. Late to bed and early to rise left me tired every day.

The pressure from the drill instructors was never-ending. One instructor was always with us and they rotated who spent the night in the barracks. I was awakened every morning by screaming and the clamor of two trashcan lids being beaten like cymbals in a nightmare band. I would still be exhausted from the previous day but couldn't linger in bed. There was no snooze option. Those trash cans would immediately send fear shooting through my body and I would jump up and fall in. Standing at attention with my toes on the centerline, I would say a silent prayer every morning that everyone made the formation on time. If the drill instructors saw anyone late or not standing at attention properly, we would all be ordered to the ready position for pushups. Cadence was called while we did pushups until everyone had surpassed their physical limitations. Eventually, we would be called back to attention and then released to prepare for morning PT. There were many days I think they made up our "mistakes" just to torture us into shape.

Challenging the physical limits of my body was obviously an important part of basic training. Most kids who enter the army are like I was, out of shape. Even those who thought they were in good shape quickly found out they weren't. Honestly, nobody could be ready for all the physical demands of basic training back then. To graduate, I had to pass every single phase, which included several physical tests. I never would have passed without being forced through all the grueling torture I was put through.

One requirement was to run two miles in fewer than nineteen minutes and five miles in fewer than fifty-five minutes. We ran every morning in formation to get fit enough to pass. Since we also needed to learn the importance of working as a team, and as a unit, our morning PT became a tool to teach this as well. A painful tool, not just for us road guards but for everyone. As we ran, there would always be some who fell out of formation. These recruits were not as fit as they needed to be and every platoon had them. Every time this happened, the formation looped back to pick up the stragglers. This made sure we finished as a platoon. The distances would gradually increase each morning, eventually getting to five miles. It tires me just thinking about those morning runs.

These runs were tough on everyone because. We knew we had to complete them in the required time if we wanted to graduate. The constant loops back to pick up stragglers frustrated all of us each morning. Listening to the drill sergeants berate and humiliate the stragglers made us angry with the few who kept causing us to turn around.

The worst result of these methods used to transform us was it also took away any feelings of sympathy we might have had, so we never considered what the stragglers felt. This isolated these poor kids and it still breaks my heart thinking back on this. These guys had volunteered to serve their country and didn't deserve to be treated as outcasts and isolated this way. To make matters worse, some guys bought into the drill instructors methodology and would berate these same guys in private. One day a drill corporal pulled a few of these idiots aside and convinced them to coordinate a "blanket party" for one particular guy.

A blanket party is the same in real-life as depicted in movies. In the darkness of night, a group of soldiers will sneak up on a fellow soldier while he is asleep. A blanket is thrown over the sleeping soldier and he is beaten. Sometimes he is pummeled with fists and kicked but usually it is done with small shovels known as entrenching tools. Sneaking in the dark while the guy is asleep and covering him with a blanket so he can't see you is cowardly. How beating a guy with a small shovel is supposed to make him a better soldier evades me.

A few of the guys approached me to participate. To the credit of my mother, I refused to be involved in this. I did convince them not to use shovels but this doesn't absolve me of the guilt and shame of not stopping or reporting it, and it shouldn't. This is a classic example of bullying and peer pressure and its negative side effects. It shows how the psychological bullying used to instill a group mentality by the drill instructors can also make you look the other way when horrible things like this happen.

Chapter 3
Basic Training

When I enlisted in the Army, I knew I would have to attend basic training and it would be hard. It's called basic training because that's exactly what it is, training on the basics of being a soldier. I learned the basic tasks necessary for all army positions while transforming physically and mentally into what a soldier was expected to be. Everything in basic training was standardized and I had to pass all of it to graduate.

The focus was on putting the fear of God in me every moment of every day, turning me into a mindless sheep. The best way to open my mind up and teach me to become a soldier was through this form of brainwashing. By putting me in an environment that wiped away all my self-worth, I became dependent on the leaders above me for direction. To do this, they kept me worn down mentally and physically and in a constant state of fear. There were no distractions other than the training I was going through.

The first few weeks of basic training was as basic as it gets. I worked on marching in formation and learning drill and ceremony procedures. I spent a lot of time in the classroom learning about being a soldier and the army regulation that now governed me. I was taught, military policies and procedures for every aspect of my new life.

I was introduced to the M16A1 rifle and taught every detail of its firing capabilities. This was the weapon assigned to every infantry soldier so I had to know it inside and out - how to break it down, clean it, assemble it, and to troubleshoot it when there were problems. I spent so much time with my rifle I could perform these tasks in my sleep. Eventually, we got to the point where we would have contests to see who could break it down and reassemble it the fastest while blindfolded.

During this period of constant fear, I quickly lost all sense of individuality and found myself looking for guidance for everything I did. Intimidated and humiliated, I blindly followed every word and command they gave me, which was the whole point.

Each day was progressively harder as I learned to be a soldier. Before I conquered one lesson, it seemed like I was moving onto the next. I was always exhausted and sore, but I knew each day was one day closer to graduation and an end to the madness. I knew if I failed to keep up with my platoon, or failed any of the qualifications, I would be recycled. Recycled meant I would be sent to a holding unit until another cycle of basic training started. I would have been assigned to the new unit and begin this whole nightmare all over again. Fear of being recycled was a powerful motivator.

Once I had learned the basic information, I began learning the skills of being an infantry soldier. I was taught how to wear a gas mask and sent to a gas chamber to experience a chemical agent firsthand. On entering, I had to hold my breath for thirty seconds before donning my mask. It was impossible to fight the burning sensation in my eyes and keep the tears from rolling down my face. I wasn't concerned with that. My main objective was simple - keep from puking.

I finally conquered the basics of the M16 rifle and got to shoot it. I learned how to zero in the sight by adjusting it to where the bullet impacted a target. I was instructed on how to fire accurately from different positions: prone, kneeling, standing, and entrenched in a foxhole. While conquering this, I was also learning about other weapons: hand grenades, claymore mines, rocket and grenade launchers, and machine guns. I had to know the nomenclature or identification number, the firing distances, impact ranges, how to assemble and disassemble them and then pass a test on all of this for each weapon. When I finally learned everything about each weapon, I got to shoot and blow stuff up with them.

I had to be taught the importance of always keeping my rifle within arm's distance. My life could depend on it so extreme measures were used to teach me this critical lesson. Humiliation was the most popular method used when a soldier misplaced his rifle. Berating trainees, forcing them to do unlimited numbers of pushups while belittling them in front of their peers was an extremely effective way to do this. One of the hardest punishments was holding my rifle in front of me with both arms outstretched and parallel to the ground. There was no quitting until they ordered it and that never seemed to happen until my arms were like noodles. The more I struggled, the more they humiliated me for being weak. The guys who continued to leave their rifles lying around had a dummy cord tied to them and their weapon to embarrass them. Of course, the rope used was always huge to ensure everyone could see it and know this was a dummy who had forgotten his rifle.

It was a sick feeling to see your drill instructor holding a rifle and realizing it was yours. One time I found myself being punished for forgetting my weapon a second time. My punishment was to squat on top of a small fence, flap my arms back and forth, and yell as loud as I could, "I am a Poo Bird!" over and over and over. Of course, I had to use a more colorful term than "poo." I can still remember the embarrassment I felt doing this while everybody laughed at me. Lesson learned. I never forgot my weapon again. I still have nightmares that I can't find my rifle.

I was introduced to combat road marching by walking between ranges and training sites. My limits were always pushed by going further and further. It seemed like I walked everywhere. Miserable, exhausted, and sore all the time, I remained completely unaware that I was getting stronger each day.

Everything we did, we did together. All of this was by design to force us to work as a platoon to instill teamwork in us. Daily competitions were set up among the platoons with the winner getting to go to chow first. Other times we competed just for the bragging rights. But teamwork wasn't the only lesson they were teaching us.

Unknowingly, I came to understand the true meaning of "esprit de corps." This wasn't simply a new phrase to memorize but something that went even deeper than words; this idea went to the core of what being a soldier in the United States military meant. It represented that unbreakable bond formed between soldiers who share the same passion for this country and a willingness to die for it. Guys working together every day as one, where there is no "me", only "us". This is a bond developed at every duty station as you remained vigilant and ready for a call to arms for your country. This was the most important thing they taught me in basic training. This bond is so strong that looking back all these years later brings back memories and emotions as vivid and powerful as the days in which they were formed.

Towards the end of basic, I had to complete a live fire exercise to give me the experience of operating in a combat environment. The exercise was done at night on an extreme obstacle course. Using different crawling techniques, I had to crawl under barbwire between covered positions, while simulating firing at targets from each position. To add realism, there was a machine gun being fired right above me the whole time using tracer bullets so I could see them. There were controlled explosions detonated all around me to create noise and confusion. I am sure this was nothing like the fear experienced in combat, but it made one heck of an impact on me.

I completed the basic portion and moved into the Advanced Individual Training (AIT) phase of basic training. There was no ceremony to mark this transition, but there was a small taste of freedom for me. As a motivator to get to this point, an overnight pass was dangled in front of the platoon as a reward. This worked well because nobody wanted to be left in the barracks while all their buddies were out having fun.

When the big night came, I got all spiffed up in my new dress uniform with my shiny rifle and grenade qualification medals on my chests and departed for town. I was confident that the ladies would be impressed when they saw me. It never occurred to me that recruits were an everyday occurrence. This was a training base after all. I would soon learn that my uniform marked me as a trainee and fresh meat to anyone wanting to take advantage of my inexperience. I was so clueless at that age.

My main objective that night, like everyone else in my platoon, was to get drunk. Very drunk. A group of us got a taxi and were driven to an area popular with trainees. ID's weren't checked because these clubs knew who their clientele was. Having just turned seventeen the previous April, I was still just a kid. Being able to enter a bar and order alcohol was a pretty big deal to me. I paid the cover price and entered, ready for whatever the night offered if alcohol was involved.

We found us a table and I ordered a beer. When the drink came, I was shocked at the ridiculously high price. Before I could complain, a group of scantily clad women came over and introduced themselves. My first reaction was *Woohoo!* I was sure that it was my uniform that attracted them to me. Being a soldier was going to have its perks. I wasn't clueless - just stupid. The beauty sitting next to me asked if I would buy her a drink. Are you kidding me? I practically ripped my pants trying to get my wallet out. Once she told the waitress what she wanted, I ordered a beer for myself. The waitress returned, passed the drinks out, and presented me with the bill. To my utter shock and disbelief, the price of my drinks was outrageous.

Looking at the ladies caused the sticker shock to wear off quickly and it wasn't long before I was coaxed into buying her another round. And then another. I no longer cared that the prices were high. There was a woman to impress. I may have been naïve back then, but I was no dummy. By the seventh or eighth round, I realized that I was being snookered. I was getting drunker and yet the scantily clad lady next to me wasn't. In fact, none of the women at the table seemed to show any signs of intoxication while all the guys were laughing and acting like fools. It occurred to me that these women worked for the club and were getting watered down drinks. This had to be a scam being run by the club. These clubs were preying on naïve recruits who were easy to spot in their dress uniforms.

Others from my platoon were beginning to have their own suspicions, so we decided to leave before we were broke. There were about eight of us and once outside we found a liquor store and pooled our money for a motel room to party in. After a few drinks, we called SFC Lee, who had given us his number in case of an emergency. Well, we had an emergency. We wanted to get drunk with him, or more precisely, get drunker with him. Drinking with the man you feared the most in the world seemed like a cool idea. Surprisingly, he accepted our drunken pleas and joined us, more out of concern for us than anything else. It was so cool seeing this godlike man, who hours earlier had us shaking in our boots, standing there drinking a beer with us.

Some of the guys were still feeling the effects of the sirens at the bar. The spells they had cast with their female guiles and skimpy clothes still held them in their grip. At some point, they decided to call an escort service. Coming from a small town, I had limited knowledge about this stuff and wanted nothing to do with it. Besides, I was too proud to pay for something I thought I could get on my own for free. It was obvious who took part in this endeavor by the screaming at the urinals. It was hilarious! We all laughed when they were marched off to see the medics and their shots of penicillin.

I spent the rest of that night of freedom drinking with my buddies and eventually fell asleep. The next morning, we were awakened by SFC Lee who calmly reminded us of our deadline to be back on post and in formation. At the designated time, SFC Lee called the platoon to attention. He then grinned and gave the command, "Right face, forward march!"

Uh oh! I thought. This wasn't going to very pleasant. I knew what was coming next. "Double time march!" Head pounding, stomach lurching, off I went on a morning run. I suspect this was to teach a lesson on overindulgence. Then again, maybe it was simply for the drill instructors pleasure.

Now that I had completed basic training, I began the Advanced Individual Training (AIT) phase. There was usually a graduation ceremony before starting AIT. In the infantry, AIT was part of my basic training. I just moved from one phase to the next and began learning my primary Military Occupational Specialty (MOS) skills and the more advanced infantry skills. During the basic training phase, we participated as a company in all training. In the AIT phase, my platoon would spend some of its time training with other 11HE9 anti-armor training platoons.

Chapter 4
AIT
Advanced Individual Training

Since AIT was still a part of basic training for infantry soldiers, there wasn't any improvement in my treatment. I remained the lowest form of life on earth spending a lot of time on my belly to remind me of this. What did change was the type of training I started to see. I began learning more advanced levels of infantry training while most days were spent learning my specific MOS. For me, this is when I learned the specifics of being a heavy anti-armor crew member.

This entailed learning the basics about the tube-launched, optically tracked, wire-guided missile system (TOW.) The TOW fired a missile that could penetrate heavy armor from a maximum range of 3,750 meters. The missile was guided by a very fine wire that unwound as the missile travels towards the target. This allowed the gunner to maintain control until the missile impacted the target.

The TOW had a large tri-pod that was anchored into the ground. A traverse was mounted on the tripod and served as the main controls for the gunner. The gunner placed each hand on knobs on the sides of the traverse to move the weapon up and down and horizontally up to 360 degrees. The launch tube that housed the missile was mounted on the front of the traverse unit and the sight used to track targets during the day was mounted on the top right. A night vision sight was mounted on top of this.

I was taught every detail the TOW and how to assemble it. I then spent time learning how to track stationary and moving targets for a long enough duration for the missile to travel and impact. The army had a targeting system that allowed me to be evaluated and scored on my ability to track targets. This would seem prehistoric to today's computer savvy kids.

To track targets and be scored, a specially designed optical sight was connected to an instructor's console. A large target panel was mounted on a rail system that allowed the target to move horizontally at a slow speed while it was tracked. The target panel had a large red plus sign painted on it with an electronic eye in its center. When the trigger was pulled, a small laser light was fired. The electronic eye communicated with the control panel the results of your tracking the target with the laser and scored you on your accuracy.

The console was used for practice and qualifying. In qualifying mode, it scored you on how long you could hold the crosshairs of the optical sight on the center of the plus sign on the target board. This wasn't as easy as it sounds when the target was moving at a quick speed.

Once I had mastered this, I began learning about the Improved Tow Vehicle (ITV) a modified armored personnel carrier. It had a dual missile launcher mounted on a turret. The turret was controlled by the gunner and could rotate 360 degrees. Mounted in a compartment on top of the launcher was the optical sight and the infrared night sight. The lower part of the turret inside the armored vehicle was the gunner's station with control panel for the entire weapon system.

Each vehicle had a four-man crew that consisted of a squad leader, a driver, a gunner, and a missile loader. As with everything in the military, there was a specific, step-by-step procedure in place for every position. Because of the hydraulic turret, the gunner had a much more detailed checklist to learn to get from the initial spotting of a target to missile impact.

A simulator of an ITV and was used for training. The training began with the gunner and loader in the passenger seat, and the instructor in the squad leaders spot. The instructor would shout, "Target in sight!" setting everyone in motion. The gunner would slide into the gunner's seat and begin his preliminary checks of the turret and hydraulics. While this was going on, the loader would slide two missiles from the rack and lay them on the vehicle floor to do a complete inspection of each one.

Once the gunner had completed checking the control panel, the turret was turned on. Grabbing both hand controls, the front of the launcher was raised while simultaneously turning the turret to the right. He stopped turning at 180 degrees so the missiles could be loaded. Once the turret stopped, the loader would open the back hatch and lock it in a partially open position which protected him from gunfire while he loaded the missiles. He would then slide both missiles into their respective tubes, lock them in place and then closed the hatch. As soon as the missiles were loaded, the squad leader would call out the degree the target was located at. The gunner would repeat the degree and prepare to turn the turret to that direction.

The loader alerted the crew when the rear hatch was closed. Upon hearing the direction, the gunner immediately turned the turret to the degree given. The gunner searched for the target through the weapon's site while turning to the degree the squad leader reported.

Once spotted, the gunner would shout, "Target acquired!" There was a specific time frame required to get from "target in sight" to "target acquired" and every squad wanted the fastest time. Everyone had to rotate between the gunner and loader positions and learn both jobs. Eventually, this would become second nature for all of us.

Once I had learned the details for working in an ITV, I practiced tracking targets using the same targeting system and tracking console we used from the ground. I had to successfully qualify with the ITV TOW system to graduate. To make the qualifying competitive, the recruit with the highest qualification would get to fire a real missile prior to graduation. I won this competition and the honor of firing the missile. I also received my first military award, a Department of Defense Certificate of Achievement. I was extremely nervous when the big day arrived because the target didn't have a big red plus sign painted on it and the missile was real. Knowing the ridicule I had endured daily, I didn't want to be the guy who missed the target and got recycled just before graduation. An unrealistic fear but one I worried about nonetheless. Fortunately, it's easy to hit a stationary target with no distractions. All I had to do was hold the crosshairs on the center mass of the target and fire the missile. It was still an awesome experience and a great way to close out my basic training.

Graduation finally came and this period of mind games and ridicule would end with it. Basic training had done what it was intended to and my time there had transformed me. I was now a soldier. No longer the carefree teenager with no direction but young man who was now part of a much bigger picture. My individuality and independent nature were stripped from me through this, replaced with discipline and a team attitude. I had volunteered to serve and defend my country and now knew what this commitment meant. I accepted it completely.

This has always been what basic training was about. These days it is nowhere near as demanding physically and mentally as it was for those of us in the early years of an all-volunteer army and at the peak of the Cold War. It can't be with everything having to be politically correct, the internet, social media, and a lawsuit-driven society. I am just as sure it wasn't as tough for me as it was for those who went before me in the age of the draft.

The army adapts to the times and basic training changes with it. We are now completely a volunteer army and a nation at war with terrorism. Kids understand this when they enlist in the military. Time is no longer spent on unnecessary exercises and tasks to break you down and rebuild you into some preconceived mold of a soldier. This allows more time to teaching recruits how to survive in this new army and against the global threats the nation faces. Most drill instructors have experienced combat in Iraq or Afghanistan and can share these experiences with trainees. Respect earned from deeds is far more powerful than respect gained through intimidation and fear. I am confident that basic training will continue to evolve as threats change.

I went through the graduation ceremony which was immediately followed by processing to my permanent duty station. I was given written orders assigning me to my unit in Germany along with airline tickets. The army was paying a $3,000 enlistment bonus to recruits who successfully completed infantry basic training. A finance office was set up as part of the out-processing to issue these bonus checks, which was substantially lower after the government took out all the taxes. I didn't have a bank account so I sent mine home to my mother.

I love my Mom so much for the way she raised me and wanted to get her something special to show her this. I decided to use part of this money to give her a gift and called home to inform her of this. Microwave ovens were just gaining popularity and a decent one cost about $1,200. I had four younger siblings she was raising alone and this was something I decided to buy her. I thought owning a microwave would make life a bit easier for my family and could think of nothing better to spend my bonus on. With some convincing, I eventually got her to agree to take what was needed from this check and buy one.

I was soon on a plane for Frankfort, Germany heading towards the start of my new life. I had no idea what to expect but was confident I was ready for it. Boy, was I in for a rude awakening.

Chapter 5
Head Start

I landed in Frankfurt, Germany and was taken to Butzbach, Germany to attend a Head Start program before being sent to my unit. The post was called Schloss Kaserne (Kaserne is the German word for barracks.) This lasted about two weeks and was designed to acclimate me to being stationed in a foreign country. I spent every morning learning the basics of speaking German. Prostitution was legal in Germany so I attended classes on symptoms and prevention of social diseases. I would be driving on German roads, so I had to learn everything about their traffic laws and how to identify all their road signs.

My time in Butzbach was exactly what I had expected army life to be like when I enlisted. The work days were from reveille (the raising of the US flag) at 6:30 am to retreat (when the flag was lowered) at 5:00 pm. The classes were scheduled from 9:00 am to 4:00 pm with most days wrapping up even earlier. My evenings were my own to do whatever I wanted and I took full advantage of this freedom.

My first evening there, I decided to scout the area and learn what a small German city was like. The downtown area was close to the post gate and consisted of a street that circled a beautiful water fountain. Around this circle, I found stores for electronics, shoes, clothing, a bakery and a grocery store. It was what you would expect in any small downtown. There were a variety of restaurants for pizza, brats, schnitzels, and a tiny one that sold gyros. The gyros were cooked on a spit in the front window that slowly turned the meat. This created an amazing aroma that lingered in the air, making it impossible to walk by without stopping. I enjoyed every one of these establishments while in Butzbach and ate many gyros late at night over the next few weeks.

Butzbach was a small town and I wanted to see everything. I saw a large building a few blocks away that appeared to have a spa and swimming pool in it. Upon further inspection, I found a sign that listed hours that it was open and times for different events. I couldn't read German so I was clueless what each event was but I did think this might be worth a return visit one evening. Then I noticed something that made me look a little closer. There appeared to be a time on Sunday evenings scheduled for nude coeds. Was I reading this right? Man, oh man, I was going to love my two years in Germany. Like any young man, I noted this time and planned to come back Sunday. In my naivety, I was sure I would meet some gorgeous German lady and get lucky. I then returned downtown to do what I had originally planned when I set out on this reconnaissance- drink.

Imagine being 17 years old, in a foreign country, and with free time on your hands to do whatever you wanted. The first thing I had learned was there was no drinking age limit in Germany and I was ready to test this out. I had noticed a bar just a few blocks from the post, near the town circle, and decided to test my new freedom there. The place was nothing special, a long bar with stools, a few tables scattered throughout, and a pool table. Just like what you would expect to find in a small local bar except this one would turn out to be quite a bit better than the average hole-in-the-wall bar.

After surveying the area, I nervously approached the bar and took a seat. The bartender quickly appeared and I proudly said, "Ein Beer!" like German was my native language.

The bartender responded, "What kind of beer would you like?"

I sheepishly replied, "Draft please."

He poured me a mug of draft and set it in front of me. I would later learn that many cities in Germany brewed their own beer so it always tasted fresh and that's what the locals drank. All I knew at that moment is I was one-month shy of my eighteenth birthday and sitting in a bar in Germany. This was even better than I hoped when I was sitting in front of that recruiter demanding Germany as my duty as- signment. Life was good!

I had just spent three months in hell having all of my self-worth and self-esteem stripped away from me. Sleep deprivation as well as physical and mental fatigue were the norm and every decision was made for me. Here I was, a few days removed from all this, and feel- ing like I had the world at my feet. I was drinking a beer and I wasn't even old enough to vote back home. Maybe this army thing was what I had hoped after all.

I drank my first German beer and boy was it good. Really good. I ordered a refill and took a closer look at my surroundings. There were only a few people here, including one other person sitting at the bar with me. Being much more confident now, I ordered a drink for him. He slid down and quickly became my best friend. I suppose free drinks can have this effect. He would become my unofficial teacher on all things German, but mostly we drank. It turned out I was a happy drunk so there was always much laughing.

One of the first things he showed me was hidden behind the bartender on the top shelf above all the hard liquor bottles. A beautifully crafted glass cowboy boot that you could order full of this delicious German beer. It must have held a half a gallon of beer. He ordered the first of what would be many boots of beer over the next few weeks.

I would frequent this establishment every night while in Butzbach and my new friend was usually there. We would drink, shoot pool and laugh. He taught me many things about Germany, most importantly the swear words. Learning a second language just isn't complete without mastering the naughty words.

My first weekend in Germany rolled around and I learned I would have both days to myself. This assignment just kept getting better. Sleeping had been a luxury taken away from me from day one so I slept in. I had no plans that day and decided to explore the town some more, besides, I needed to find a swimsuit for Sunday's spa plans. I wanted to be prepared in case I had interpreted the sign wrong. I sure didn't want to get arrested for public indecency. How do you tell your mom you were arrested your first week in Germany for entering a public pool commando style? I headed out on my second recon but this time I went in many of the stores and browsed around. After spending a few hours doing this, I headed back towards the bar, swimsuit in hand, to meet up with my new German friend.

I knew in advance he would be there. We had planned on meeting up here. The plan for the rest of the day was simple- drink lots of beer. He had a different plan because it was the weekend and he was off from work. Beer was for work nights it seemed. This is when I was introduced to cognac. He ordered us both a cognac and coke and I found my second favorite drink for the next few years. I quickly ordered a bottle of cognac and a two-liter bottle of Coke. When the bartender sat down the bottles, the first thing I noticed was the pretty red rose on the cognac label that gave the bottle a classy look. I noticed the Coke bottle looked just like it did back home but when I poured it there wasn't much fizz. I never found out why but every Coke I bought locally would be like this.

Now here is the thing about drinking cognac- it is nothing like beer. With beer, the more you drink the drunker you get. Or in my case, the sillier you get. You can always feel the alcohol take effect and can usually tell when it's time to quit and go to bed. Not with cognac- at least not this cognac. If I was sitting still I could feel a slight buzz, but the real effect didn't hit me until I started moving around. The two of us finished this bottle off and, well, that's it. I don't remember anything else from the night. The only thing I know for certain is I somehow managed to get back to post and make it to the right room. I woke up the next morning in my assigned bed with one of the worst hangovers I have ever had.

I was young and even this wasn't going to ruin my day. I had a date with a spa full of naked women waiting for me that evening. I spent most of the day lying around and as the day wore on, the more normal I felt and the more nervous I got. The magic hour finally arrived and I grabbed my swimsuit and a towel, just in case, and headed out the gate to the pool. The sun was getting ready to set at it was getting cold. I arrived and entered the building where there was an elderly woman sitting at a table with a cash box. My mind was now racing with all kinds of wild thoughts. What do I say? How do I tell her I am here for the coed nude swimming? What if I was wrong? It was obvious I was an American soldier. I nervously approached and asked, "How much?" and pointed to the sign. She told me the amount and I paid. Just like that, I was on my way to paradise.

By now I was anxious to see naked women and I hurriedly entered the men's locker room. I looked around and instantly noticed very few men. This was a good sign because it meant more naked women for me. Yep, things were looking good for Private Kern. I found an empty locker and quickly discarded my clothes. I found the door to the pool and made my way towards it, naked and nervous.

The first room I entered was a small weight room with a couple of treadmills, a few weight machines and some free weights, things typically found in a small gym. What I didn't expect to find was all old men and women, some modestly covered with a towel and some completely naked in their full glory for all to see. More disturbing was the fact that they were working out like it was the most natural thing in the world. Not a pretty sight. It didn't take me long to make a hasty retreat to explore the rest of the facility and see what it had to offer. Of course, my primary mission was to find more naked women, preferably younger ones. I found a sauna room, a steam room, a couple massage rooms, a small indoor pool, and a small outdoor pool. And all were being used by naked old people. Mostly women, but still old. Not what I expected at all. There I was, a physically fit young man strolling among these naked old people.

Suddenly, feeling like a pervert, I tried not to stare or make eye contact. I wanted it to look like I wasn't there just to see naked women which was not an easy thing to do. It felt like every eye in the place was now on me. Older women or not, they were still naked women, so

I felt obligated to stay a while longer. In truth, I doubt anybody even noticed me.

Now that my original plans were a train wreck, I decided to make the best of the situation and enjoy the fitness options in the club. I had absolutely no desire to try the weight room. Seeing old people lifting weights in the raw was not a pretty sight and not so easy to forget. I spent time in the sauna and steam room with them but I avoided the lower benches. The last thing I wanted was to turn around and, well, see anything old and wrinkled staring back at me. I also swam in the tiny indoor pool and utilized the whirlpool. For precautionary reasons, I occasionally swam in the freezing outdoor pool. But only one quick lap. I wasn't that tough. One of the things I had just learned in the Head Start program was that Germany is geographically like Oregon in location and it is very frigid there in early March.

The next week I continued my military orientation classes on post during the day and my German orientation classes in the bar at night. Most of this time was spent drinking beer and playing pool. Back then, playing pool was a popular bar activity and there was always someone playing. If I wanted to play, I laid a quarter on the side to signal I wanted to play the winner. If there were others also waiting, then there would be a row of quarters lying there and you placed your quarter down at the end of the line. I became quite familiar to the local patrons, which tends to happen after spending so much time with them. Some nights it was just me and my German buddy, and those were my favorite nights since we spent more time drinking and laughing than shooting pool.

I spent my final night in Butzbach with my German buddy drinking. I bought a bottle of cognac and tore the rose off the bottle and put it in my wallet between my German and American bills. The next thing I remember is waking up in a very dark, musty place with steel bars over one of the doors like some sort of dungeon. This would have been a pretty frightening image to encounter under normal circumstances but was even more so considering I had no idea where I was and no recollection of how I got there.

It turns out I had managed to find my way to the basement of my building. The barracks I was staying in looked like an old medieval castle and had survived two World Wars and God knows what else. It seemed like I had a knack for getting back on the base and in the right building when I was drunk. This time I obviously went downstairs instead of up and crawled under the stairs to sleep. I later learned the barred doors led to the unit armory and not a cell.

My head was screaming and my stomach was churning as I pulled out my pocket watch. Seeing the time, I realized it was late morning and I was supposed to be loading the bus shortly for the transfer to my permanent duty station.

Head pounding, I raced upstairs to my room. I quickly packed my stuff and ran back downstairs to report in. While waiting for the van to arrive with no memories of the previous evening, I decided to check my wallet and make sure I hadn't spent all my money. Tucked between my currencies were three paper roses. No wonder I woke up in the basement.

Eventually, I loaded up on the bus to head towards the next phase of my German adventure. I was starting to feel a little better as the bus left Schloss Kaserne. As the bus made its way through the streets of Butzbach, my mind began to wander, reliving my many activities these past two weeks. This was going to be an awesome two years in Germany.

Chapter 6
The Rock
Ayers Kaserne
Kirch-Goens, West Germany

I was assigned to the Anti-Tank Platoon, Combat Support Company, 3rd Battalion 36th Infantry Regiment of the 1st Brigade, 3rd Armor Division. The 1st Brigade was in Kirch-Goens and consisted of two Armor battalions, two Mechanized Infantry Battalions, and one Military Police platoon. The 3rd Battalion had three Infantry Companies, (Alpha, Bravo, and Charlie Company), Headquarters Company (all the battalion staff personnel and medics) and my unit, the Combat Support Company (CSC). My company was made up of four platoons, headquarters platoon, scout platoon, a mortar platoon, and the antitank platoon. I was unaware of any of this at the time. This Kaserne was known as Ayers Kaserne and was nicknamed "The Rock."

I was nervous as we approached the main gate, but mostly I was still sick from the cognac. Looking out the window I couldn't help but get excited. The entrance to the post had this large arch above it with the words "AYERS KASERNE" and "US ARMY" above that. Beyond the gate were uniform rows of buildings that left no doubt this was a military installation. I could just feel all the history screaming at me as we drove through the gate. It's hard to put into words all the emotions I felt, but pride would have to be at the top of the list.

A small shack stood at the gate with a single MP standing in the center of the road. He was directing traffic in and out, focusing on making sure those who entered were military and checking identification when necessary. I passed through this gate and traveled a short distance before reaching my destination. I unloaded my gear from the bus and got directions to my unit.

I walked the short distance to my company and reported in as instructed. I was informed that my unit was "in the field," a term used to mean out for extended training, and would return in a few days. I was then introduced to the Non-commissioned Officer in Charge (NCOIC) who took me to my room.

The barracks was an old three story building. The first floor was the admin area with offices for the company commander, executive officer, first sergeant, and each platoon sergeant and platoon leader. There was a large recreation room that had a pool table, television, and pinball machines. The supply room and armory were in the basement. The second and third floors were divided by the stairs in the middle and each platoon was assigned to its own section.

The bathroom and showers were located at the center of each floor, across from the stairwell doors. Entering the bathroom, there were rows of sinks and mirrors running down the left and right walls and old boiler radiators that provided heat to the barracks under the windows on the far walls. An entryway to the left accessed the showers, which was a large open room with a row of showers running down the walls just like in basic. The room to the far right had a row of urinals along one wall and toilets on the opposite wall. The toilets were divided by stalls and even had a door for each one- a sight for sore eyes for those of us coming straight out of basic training.

My platoon was assigned to the section to the left on the third floor. I was taken to the second to last room on the left and told this was the room for my squad. Entering the room, I saw one bed to the left of the door, a bunk bed on the far right and an empty bed and locker on the far left. Since my unit was deployed, I was given my first weekend at the Rock to do as I pleased. I unpacked, made my bed and set up my locker like I had been trained to do. I was still feeling pleased with my choice of Germany.

I decided to take a stroll around the post and acclimate myself. Close to the barracks was the mess hall and a very short distance away I found the motor pool. It had a single row of long buildings running along the far side with large bay area inside where the vehicles were worked on that served as the maintenance garages. Gazing farther down the motor pool area, I could see row after row of tanks and other armored vehicles. The most intriguing thing was the actual parking area for these vehicles. It wasn't concrete or asphalt but small stones evenly laid for the entire motor pool.

Continuing my exploration, I walked back towards brigade headquarters where I had first been dropped off.   I wandered through other battalion areas seeing more barracks exactly like mine. I came across a large building which housed the PX, snack bar, commissary and a small bank. I felt confident I could now find my way around and headed into the commissary. I had decided to buy a cooler and a case of Budweiser to ice overnight. I still couldn't believe I could buy alcohol at seventeen years old. The belief among soldiers was that if we were old enough to serve our country and possibly die for it, then we were old enough to drink. And we drank a lot.

The next morning was Saturday; I arose early and headed towards the mess hall. I was pleasantly surprised when I reached the chow line to see a cook in front of a large grill making omelets. There was also a nice selection of other breakfast choices but it was the omelets that kept my attention. Life was looking good for this soldier.

With a full belly and feeling like I had the world by the tail, I headed back to my room. Since I had nothing else to do, I decided to start drinking and popped the tab on an ice-cold Budweiser. By early afternoon, I was toasted and passed out. The next day I awoke feeling miserable. With a hangover and nothing to do, I spent the entire day in my bed reading and sleeping. My Aunt Nancy had ignited a passion in me to read just before I enlisted that continues even now. I would become a huge reader in Germany and spend many off days in bed reading while the effects of the previous night's drinking wore off. On this morning, I recovered in my room alone, clueless to what was ahead of me. Soon, I would see the real picture of what being stationed in Germany was like during this period of the Cold War.

My unit returned from training the next day. I was sent to the motor pool to meet my section leader, SSG Turnbow, who then introduced me to Frank and Walter, the other members of my squad and my roommates. I would meet my third roommate later. His name was Reggie and he drove the other vehicle in my section. I was told to help them as they unpacked their equipment and gear and began the process of recovery. This wasn't the best of circumstances to meet the guys I could go to war with. Here they were, just back from training, and they were cold, dirty, and tired while I was freshly showered and wearing my new, clean pressed fatigues and shiny boots. To make matters worse, my training was on the Improved TOW Vehicle (ITV). They were cleaning an old Armored Personnel Carrier (APC) with the TOW mounted on a pedestal. This looked ancient, and I had no idea where to help or what do.

My new crew members referred to me as "newbie" in a somewhat bitter tone as they told me where to help. I couldn't really argue with this title since I was only a few weeks removed from basic training. Walter was the current gunner and was cleaning in the back of the vehicle. Our driver, Frank, was spending an awful lot of time climbing into the engine compartment with a rag. When I asked him about this, he explained that the recovery part of training was worse than the training itself. Everything had to be spotless from the vehicle and weapon system to your personal weapon and gear. I soon learned just how right he was.

A few days after returning from every training deployment came the dreaded inspections. All my personal training gear, rucksack, sleeping bag, canteens, and so forth had to be laid out in a specific way and was checked for cleanliness. Then came the formations outside, in front of the barracks, where we stood at attention while the company commander moved down the lines inspecting our rifles. And lastly came the dreaded motor pool inspection. The loading ramp at the rear of the vehicle was down and the engine panels opened. All the equipment was laid out behind the vehicle. The battalion commander conducted these inspections and he was a small, thin, gray-haired lieutenant colonel and apparently, a clean freak. I now understood why Frank had spent so much time climbing around the engine compartment. The battalion commander would thoroughly inspect each vehicle and pieces of equipment. When it came time to inspect the engine, he would slip on a white glove and climb right up into the engine compartment looking for dirt. I couldn't believe what I was seeing.

This was how life was for a soldier stationed in West Germany during the Cold War. Units deployed for extended training, recovered from the deployment and prepared for the next deployment. And on the rare occasions you weren't preparing or recovering, you trained on post. Everything I did was to prepare me for a Soviet invasion. It was a real threat and I had to be ready for it every minute of every day.

Physical fitness was a necessity in the infantry, and just like basic training, it was done every day. Monday, Wednesday and Friday was company PT and on Tuesdays and Thursdays it was done as a platoon. I had to be tested every six months to make sure I continued to meet the military's fitness requirements. The minimum requirements to pass were forty pushups in two minutes, forty sit-ups in two minutes, and I had to be able to run two miles in eighteen minutes or less. These were just minimum standards and I didn't want to be the guy who barely squeaked by so I had to take PT seriously.

Everyone had to be present and accounted for by reveille at 6:30 am. After reveille, the company marched to its designated area to conduct PT. Calisthenics were conducted for about thirty minutes before running. These runs were usually around five miles and always in formation. Most of the time I ran on roads throughout the post but occasionally the commanders would take the formation off post to run on the roads and fields just outside the gate. The run would end where it started with a few more sets of pushups done for good measure. Everyone from commander to private was winded and exhausted at the end of PT. I was then released to shower and eat until the 9:00 AM company formation.

Physical fitness had to be maintained year round no matter what the temperature and conditions were outside. The army issued me different uniforms designated to accommodate the seasonal weather changes. I wore yellow PT shorts and a white T-shirt with the unit logo on days that were warm enough and my fatigue pants and olive drab T-shirt along with sneakers on cold weather days. In cold weather and snow, I wore my complete fatigues with the shirts untucked and my combat boots. It would have been impossible to run and keep the shirt tucked in.

I was assigned to an armored division with an armored vehicle to transport me and the rest of my squad but I was still in the infantry. I always had to be prepared to perform my job without the luxury of a vehicle. We were called grunts for a reason. They took this very seriously and marched me at every opportunity they could. We usually traveled in a staggered formation requiring us to marching single file on both sides of the road. I had to maintain a specific distance from the person in front of me while keeping centered between the two soldiers on the opposite side of the road. I kept my weapon pointed towards the terrain on my side of the road while I scanned for any possible enemy activity. The further along I marched, the harder it was to keep the required spacing.

As difficult as this was, the required twelve-mile forced marches were pure torture. I had to be able to complete this in less than three hours in full combat gear, a forty-pound ruck sack and my rifle. This was an individual qualification so I didn't have to worry about staying in formation while I struggled to complete it. We would all be lined up at a starting point with a marked route of twelve miles in front of us. Every soldier had his own plan for completing the course. Plans varied but I tried to sprint out the gate for as long as I could, walk to catch my breath, then sprint or speed march some more. All plans were discarded quickly and I found myself just stumbling along, knowing I couldn't finish under three hours by just walking but helpless to go much faster. I had no choice but to force myself to pick up the pace as often as I could.

Unlike the unit road marches, here I found myself walking all alone, with nothing to distract me but the pain and fatigue that overwhelmed me. This resulted in my mind thinking about nothing but the brutality of the road march, making this a mental challenge as well. With no indications of how far I had gone, time seemed to stop. Fear would creep in that I wasn't going to finish in the required time and I would try to run more. After a few steps of running, my body would remember the pain and revert to walking.

Nothing mattered but reaching the end and God forbid I failed. This meant my buddies would have ridiculed me, and worse yet, I would have to repeat this torturous march in a few days. So, I slithered on with a zombie-like shuffle, dragging one leg forward and then the other, slowly moving forward. About three quarters into the march, I could sense the finish line and a small burst of adrenaline would give me a burst of energy. I would pick up my pace for a few minutes and then it was gone. Over and over, jog then shuffle, eventually I crossed the finish line and I was done. Half crawling to the side of the road, I fell to the ground and laid on my back. My muscles screaming so badly I thought I might be dying, I laid there until somebody yelled at me to get up.

A confrontation with the Soviets would have involved the use of chemical and biological weapons. We knew they had them and would use them so we prepared for it. There was a gas chamber, just like in basic training, that was used to practice the proper wear of the mask. It also served as a reminder to everyone how it felt to be exposed to a chemical agent.

On April 16th, 1981, barely over a month since reporting to my unit, I was at this chamber. When it was my turn, I filled my lungs as full of air as I could and entered the chamber. My eyes immediately began burning while I stood there holding my breath until instructed to put on my gas mask. I waited to have the seal checked to confirm that I had donned it properly before getting permission to exit the chamber. Once outside, with eyes burning and tears rolling heavily down my face, I yanked off my mask. I desperately fought to keep my breakfast down while gasping for that breaths of fresh air. The last thing I wanted to do was give Frank something else to tease this newbie about.

While I had been waiting to enter the chamber, I realized it was my 18th birthday. I had been so busy learning and trying to fit in, I had completely lost track of the date. It was easy for this to happen since dates weren't an important part of my life anymore. The only date anyone cared for was the date we were scheduled to depart from Germany. The training and hardships I went through were so demanding that I knew why everyone couldn't wait to leave Germany. Every one of us kept track of the number of days until we got on that plane. This wasn't exactly how I would have envisioned spending this milestone birthday. It's not surprising how quickly the army had changed my priorities and that my birthday could so easily be forgotten. It wasn't a big deal to me anymore. I now had more important things to worry about than birthdays. I must admit that it did turn out to be my most memorable birthday. Few people get gassed on the day they turn eighteen.

The following month, the company decided to hold a competition for soldier of the month. Nobody was volunteering for this so as the newbie with barely two months in country, I was ordered to represent the platoon. I wasn't exactly overjoyed about this but the reward of a four-day pass seemed like a nice excuse to try and win the thing. I would later learn that three and four day passes were common and the entire unit was given them after most extended training deployments. Unaware of this, I prepared in earnest to win this competition. I spent every spare moment I had memorizing manuals and standards and procedures to prepare for this. Current events proved to be a bit difficult to study because the only news available was in the Stars and Stripes newspaper. There was a military television channel called the Armed Forces Network (AFN) but there was only one television in the building and it was in the rec room.

The first sergeant and platoon sergeants made up the board. Each of them had specific categories of questions to ask. These questions ranged from weapons specifications, military history, chain of command personnel, current events and military policies and procedures. I reported in full dress uniform, cleaned, pressed, and brass shining, and my first sergeant inspected and evaluated my appearance. He then directed me to sit and face the board and each of them then took turns grilling me with questions from their categories.

As luck would have it, I won.

My pride in this accomplishment would be short-lived. It would become yet another tool for the platoon to tease and torment this newbie with.

When I wasn't being pushed to my limits physically, I trained on my specific job. My unit was expecting the ITV's to arrive a few months after I got there. I trained on the APC to ensure I remained proficient at my job until it got there. The Soviets weren't going to hold off an invasion while we waited for the modernized vehicles. I would march down to the motor pool and practice going from spotting a target to having the missile system up and the target in sight just like I did in AIT. Except this TOW was mounted on a pedestal and everything was done manually. We would take turns as the gunner and missile loader, competing against each other for the best times. Frank and

I were like oil and water, a fact not lost on Walter, so these competitions were always heated with Walter good-naturedly pushing the right buttons to get me and Frank fired up. We never came to blows but there were times we came close. Walter just stood back laughing, enjoying the strife he had created.

Just when I felt like I had finally mastered the obsolete APC, the ITV's arrived. I was one of the few already trained on it giving me a leg up on the platoon for the first time while they trained and qualified. This put an end to the newbie title for me and it felt good. Frank would still call me newbie, usually after some prodding from Walter because he knew how it irritated me. Oil and Water.

Training became intense and it felt like I spent every waking moment inside my vehicle. Because of my experience with the new ITV, I was assigned as the gunner of my squad. The training wasn't limited to the new hydraulic turret but covered every position in the new vehicle. Our mission was critical so it was important that this happen quickly, and it did.

As the gunner, I would be responsible for taking out Soviet armored vehicles. It was important that I recognize every vehicle I would encounter on the battle field. I had a deck of cards I used to memorize every NATO and Eastern Bloc vehicle. There was a picture of a vehicle on one side of the card and information about it on the other. I had to identify each vehicle as friendly or enemy, and know the capabilities of each one as well. The last thing I wanted to do was fire a missile at a friendly tank. We all took our jobs very serious and spent a lot of our personal time reviewing and testing each other with these cards. We never knew when this knowledge would be put to the real test but we were ready.

The base had a small indoor theater where my platoon conducted live fire training with our rifles. There was a room inside where movies of different combat situations were projected onto a small white screen. Right behind this was another white screen with a light directed at the back of it all. There was a dirt bank behind the screens that stopped the bullets that were fired at the screen. I had to lay in a prone firing position and shoot at enemy soldiers as they appeared on screen. The bullet holes made in the screen would allow the light from behind to shine through and I could immediately tell if I hit the target.

We also used the theater to practice targeting and tracking Soviet tanks with the TOW system. A special optical sight was used that projected a small red laser onto the screen. A battle scene with Soviet

44

tanks was projected on the screen. Since the TOW missiles were wire-guided, this training made it possible to simulate tracking targets until missile impact. I had to place the crosshairs on the center of a tank and keep them there while it moved around the battlefield. The laser allowed me to be scored and to give me a realistic idea of just how difficult it was to hold a moving target center mass long enough for the missile to hit it. This training would seem prehistoric to soldiers now, but in 1981 it was pretty high tech to me.

The possibility of encountering chemical and nuclear attacks from a Soviet invasion was very high during this time. In fact, a nuclear war was one of the biggest fears in the world during this period of the Cold War. To prepare for a nuclear explosion, I was taught to lie down facing away from the blast, "ass to the blast" as it was called, with my rifle underneath my body. I knew there was no way I would survive a nuclear bomb but I guess the army thought this would make it easy to identify me as soldier once the radiation levels were safe. I would be one of the silhouettes burnt on the ground, in a straight line, facing away from the impact area.

Nuclear, biological, and chemical (NBC) attacks were possible so we always had to be ready for this. MOPP training was incorporated into all our training, and into everything we did. There was a chemical warning system in place known as Mission Oriented Protection Posture level (MOPP). This would warn us of the level of threat for chemical or biological agent agents. There were four warning levels that ranged from MOPP Level 1 to MOPP Level 4. Level one was for mild risk of exposure and required wearing the jacket and pants. Level 4 required wearing all my protective gear. My chemical gear included a chemical protective jacket and pants worn over boots and protective gloves, and the protective mask and hood. The pants and jacket were made of a cotton material and lined with carbon to protect my body from most chemical and biological agents. The gear was very warm and heavy so it slowed even the most basic tasks down. I came to hate my MOPP gear and dreaded MOPP 4 training.

The likelihood of the Soviets using chemical and biological agents was so strong that all the training I went through was conducted in protective gear. I moved up and down the different levels as ordered by my chain of command. The absolute worst thing I had to do in MOPP gear was the road marches. It was difficult enough conducting them in full combat gear but it was brutal marching in MOPP gear. I would tire almost immediately, becoming numb to everything around me, thinking of nothing but taking that next step, then the one after that, until finally reaching the end. We didn't march very far in full gear because of this.

Heat exhaustion was always a major concern during training and was an even bigger concern when training in MOPP gear. It was imperative that I know the symptoms to look for in myself and others and always be on the lookout for these signs. Water was always available and I had to drink lots of it as a preventative measure. All of this was necessary to ensure I could perform all my duties efficiently in a contaminated environment.

The time came to begin preparations for the annual deployment to Grafenwoehr and Hohenfels. Every vehicle had to be driven down to the post railhead and loaded and strapped down onto flatbed train cars. All weapon systems and personal gear was secured in large containers and loaded as well. Since the barracks would be empty and locked, my locker had to be banded shut. This annual pilgrimage was for roughly thirty days of intense training. The first half of training was conducted at Grafenwoehr and then we would convoy to Hohenfels for the next few weeks before returning by train to the Rock.

I made many of these deployments while I was stationed in Germany. One of my favorite memories of this annual trek is from my second year. Preparations were completed with the loading of the vehicles and equipment the night before departing. I had the evening free and so I did what young soldiers usually did with time to kill back then- I drank. At some point in time, somebody made the boneheaded decision to buy picnic tables for the soldiers stationed in Germany. I guess they thought one of us might be overcome with the urge to make sandwiches and invite other guys to have a picnic when we weren't training. Outside, each company had a common area with two or three picnic tables. In all my time there, I don't recall anybody sitting at those tables. Well, boys will be boys and in the wee hours of the morning somebody came up with the idea to carry every picnic table in the battalion down to the railhead and put them on top of the vehicles on the train.

So there we were, a bunch of giggling, drunk soldiers toting picnic tables through the post. Somehow we managed to get every one of them moved without getting caught. Not one MP or any of the company CQ's saw us. Imagine waking up to the sight of a train full of armored vehicles lined up with a bunch of picnic tables on them. We thought it was hilarious and returned to our rooms anxious to see the reactions in the morning.

I awoke the next morning still intoxicated from my late night of drinking. In remembering what we had done the night before, the surge of fear that followed instantly sobered me up. I went to formation and everyone was talking and laughing about the incident and I was certain we would all be busted for our mischievousness. The commanders didn't seem to share the humor in our little excursion the night before and made all sorts of threats to the culprits. I was so terrified of getting caught that I didn't tell anyone about my involvement and was unable to share in the laugh our antics caused. Apparently, none of the other guys bragged about their involvement either, because we were never caught.

Chapter 7
Cold War

The world feared communism and its military state and dictatorships. The United States and the USSR represented both sides of this struggle between freedom and tyranny. In the war against Hitler and his Nazi regime, the Soviet Union and the United States found themselves on the same side of the fence. Towards the end of the war, the Soviet Union advanced on the Nazis from the east while the United States and allied forces advanced from the west. The big fear at the time was that these two forces that despised each other would eventually meet in Germany and nobody wanted that to happen.

After World War II in 1945, Germany was divided into two countries with the larger western portion becoming the Federal Republic of Germany and the smaller eastern area became the German Democratic Republic (GDR). The west was then divided into three sectors to be controlled by the occupying countries at the end of the war - the US, Britain and France, while the east would be under the control of the Soviet Union. The former capital city of Berlin was located completely within the GDR and was similarly divided into sections with the eastern half of the city controlled by the Soviets and the western half by the US, Britain and France. Years later, the Soviets would build the Berlin Wall which surrounded the NATO side of Berlin, resulting in further isolation from both East Germany and its allies in the west.

Shortly after World War II, the U.S. found itself battling the growth of communism in the Korean War (1950-1954). Immediately after this, communism would get a foothold in Northern Vietnam. In 1961, the United States began significantly expanding its role, becoming actively involved by 1965. An extremely unpopular war back home, troops would eventually get pulled out in 1973. Saigon would fall in 1975 when the communist north completely took control of the country. While the United States had been spending huge amounts of money in these conflicts, the Soviet Union was putting most of its resources into growing its military into the largest in the world.

The United States and its NATO allies maintained a nuclear arsenal larger than that of the Warsaw Pact during the early years of the Cold War. The United States followed a military strategy known as the Mutually Assured Destruction (MAD) doctrine. The basic premise of this doctrine was the belief that if both sides had enough nuclear weapons, neither would use them out of fear of retaliation from the other. A full nuclear war would wipe out both sides, negating any advantage from the use of nuclear weapons. This nuclear dominance had shifted to the Soviets by the end of the Vietnam War, shifting the balance of power and making the threat of a nuclear war a real concern.

The General Defense Plan (GDP) was implemented as part of our Cold War strategy and laid out measures to protect Europe in the event of a Soviet invasion. West Germany would have a significant role in these plans since it bordered communist East Germany and Czechoslovakia. It was determined by military leaders that an area in Western Germany near the town of Fulda had the most likely terrain the Soviets would use to move their huge armored divisions through if they were going to invade. This area was known as the Fulda Gap. The 3rd Armored Division was located at various posts in Western Germany and was tasked with the responsibility of defending this gap until our European allies could get there.

Communism didn't grow through elections but by force. This is why the Soviets put so much money into growing their military during the cold war. World War II was still recent history and the ease that Hitler had been able to conquer Europe was fresh in everyone's mind. A Soviet invasion into Europe and the spread of communism could not be allowed to happen. If this occurred, it would lead to World War III, and inevitably a nuclear war.

Since an invasion was more likely to come without warning, the military had an alarm system in place in Europe known simply as "alerts. The alerts were designed to ensure the readiness of all units to deploy rapidly in the event of a Soviet attack. There were two types of alerts I had to be ready for. The first was the muster alert which only required that I return to my unit and sign in within two hours of the alert activation. The second was the full combat readiness alert which gave me four hours from activation to be ready for deployment. I had to have all my gear and weapons loaded in my vehicle and be in my assigned position ready to mobilize. No matter where I went or what I was doing, I had to be ready for this.

Alerts could be given from division, brigade, or battalion level at any time. They were sometimes activated when there was a scheduled deployment, and once everyone was accounted for we would depart. To ensure unit readiness and remind us of the seriousness of our jobs, there were unexpected alerts where I would roll out the back gate to a designated location and then return to post that same day. A few times this happened, I remained deployed for a couple days of training before returning to The Rock. Everything was designed to keep soldiers on their toes and remind us of the seriousness of our mission. I rarely knew in advance when one would happen and I certainly never knew when one was activated whether it was a test or the real thing. I did know it was not pleasant if the time requirements for these alerts were not met.

On March 30, 1981, the alert notification was given in the wee hours of the morning. I quickly grabbed all my gear and reported to the motor pool with the rest of the guys. Once everything was fully loaded on the vehicle, I got into my assigned position and waited for the "all clear" to be given. I became more and more nervous as each minute passed. Finally, the order came, but not the one I had expected. Instead, I was told to form up in company formation right there in the motor pool.

Not a good sign.

I stood there nervously while the company commander blistered us for not meeting the deadline. Once he released us, I was chastised again by my platoon sergeant in much more colorful language before being released to begin the process of unpacking.

Later that day, I learned that President Reagan had been shot. The only source I had for major news was AFN which had a radio and TV station. I watched some of the news updates on the TV in the Rec Room. The room was packed with nervous young men anxious for news on the president. The entire unit seemed to have remained in the building that day, closely following the news.

Every room in the barracks had at least one huge stereo system in it. Most weekends there was always a variety of music blasted throughout the barracks as rooms battled to see whose system was the loudest. On this day, every radio was tuned to AFN to hear updates on the attempted assassination. Unlike today, news was more controlled as it was released to the public. It was even slower when there was only the one source for news leading to all sorts of speculation and rumors traveling through the barracks. The most believable rumor was that the Soviets were behind this. Since we had been groomed to hate the Soviets, there was a lot of chest beating going on and talk of how we were going to kick their communist butts for this. When I went to bed, I still had no news confirming who was behind this assassination attempt so I went to sleep confident that the Soviets had carried out this unfathomable attack on our president.

While I slept that night, the full combat alert order was sounded again. Immediately wide awake, I began the task of loading my vehicle and preparing for combat. The silence throughout the barracks was unsettling. Absent was the small talk, laughter, or any of the usual conversations that normally occurred. I made my way to the motor pool and the silence seemed even quieter-if that's possible. The air was heavy with the fear everyone felt. I just knew deep down that I was being sent to fight the Soviets. Locked and loaded in my armored vehicle, I waited nervously for the order to roll out. I have never been more scared in my life yet, at the same time, I was ready and committed to teaching the Soviets a lesson.

I silently sat there, we all sat there, each of us with our own thoughts and fears going through our heads as we waited. Finally, the order came to stand down. Shocked, I exited my vehicle anxious to learn what had just happened. No information was forthcoming so I began the process of recovery. Eventually, I heard that the alert order had been a mistake. This was supposed to have been a muster alert but had erroneously been passed down the chain of command as a full combat alert. Needless to say, there were a lot of unhappy people upon learning this. Unhappy, but relieved. The only consolation was the knowledge that somewhere a lieutenant was getting a good butt chewing for messing this up.

The bottom line here is that this was the reason why the United States maintained a presence in West Germany during the Cold War. As a soldier, I quickly learned this when I arrived there. This is what I trained for every day. The likelihood of a Soviet invasion during the early 1980's was probably at its highest level and I was a part of the first line of defense. I had to be ready.

Chapter 8
GAFB
German Armed Forces Badge
Bronze Schutzenschnur

The German version of the army's Expert Infantry Badge (EIB) was the Schutzenschnur, the German Armed Forces Badge (GAFB). I was extremely fortunate to be able to participate in the testing process for this award. Arrangements were made for my unit to go through the exact same qualification process that the German soldiers did. The qualifications were very similar to ours, except they had three different levels of qualification giving the distinction of a gold, silver, or bronze award. And, like our version, this was a very demanding process to complete and pass for this honor.

Some of the tests were just pass or fail, but most had the gold, silver, or bronze standards to meet. If I failed to meet the minimum requirements for one task, I would have failed the qualification for the award. Each event with gold, silver, and bronze rankings was scored. After completing all the events, these scores were averaged to determine overall rankings. Everyone went through the entire process whether they passed or not but I went into the process hoping to get the award. I wanted it, and planned to get it. The entire qualification was done over a couple of days.

One of the first things I had to complete was the 100-meter swim in fatigues within four minutes or less. I wore my PT uniform of gym shorts and t-shirt underneath my fatigues. After completing the swim, I had to tread water while removing my fatigues without using the side of the pool for support.

Then came the track and field portion of the test. We were split up into groups and rotated around the track to be tested in the different events. There was an 11 x 10-meter sprint that had to be run in a maximum time of sixty seconds for the bronze, and forty-two seconds or less for the gold. The Flex Arm Hang was an odd test that required me to pull myself up on a chin up bar and hold this upward position without my chin touching the bar. This had a minimum time of five seconds for bronze and sixty-five seconds for gold. Another event was the 1000 meter run which had a maximum finish time of six minutes and thirty seconds for the bronze. The gold qualification for this was three minutes and forty-five seconds or less. There was also a long jump and shot put event.

Next came the marksmanship qualifications with the 9-mm pistol used by the Germans, which was very similar to the .45 caliber pistol we used. The pistols were loaded with six rounds that were fired at a silhouetted target twenty-five meters away. Two rounds were fired from each of the three standard firing positions - a prone position lying on the ground, a kneeling position with one knee on the ground, and standing straight up. All six shots had to land inside the target for gold, five hits for silver, and four hits for the bronze qualification level.

The final event was the hardest, a twenty-kilometer road march in three hours or less. Twenty kilometers is a little over twelve miles and it had to be completed carrying a rifle and a full ruck sack. Even though I trained hard for this road march, the time limit made it overwhelming. By now, I was in extremely good condition, physically and mentally, and could easily walk the distance, the difficulty was having to complete it in under three hours. No matter how fit I was or how fast I walked, I would still have to run for large sections to be able to meet the time requirement. Because of this, at some point in the road march, fatigue started creeping in, slowing me down and making it even more difficult to finish. Once I started getting tired, it became harder to distract myself from this grueling task, making this a mental test as well. I started thinking about the difficulty of finishing and doubts began creeping into my thoughts. This is what the time limit was designed to do, to challenge my mental stamina along with my physical fitness, both important parts of being an efficient infantry soldier.

To offset the difficulty of the road march, two of my friends and I devised a plan to work together. Our plan was simple, stay together, keep each other motivated, and push each other to the finish line. It was a good plan and it worked for about two hours. When the event started, we sprinted for the first half mile or so, putting us towards the front of the group. We then alternated walking and trotting for as long as we could (which wasn't very long) before we were huffing and puffing for fresh air. We then decided walking at a fast pace was a better idea. This plan worked for a while as well. I was able to walk at a brisk pace with my friends and remain at the front of the pack. To divert our minds from the pain of the march, we talked about everything that came to mind, sang our favorite songs (including a few military ones), and told lots of jokes to distract our thoughts from the demands being made on our bodies. I am sure we were quite the site, singing and laughing along those German roads that day.

Eventually, the physical demands became too much to ignore and overwhelmed me, leading to longer and longer periods of silence. It became difficult to concentrate. Then the real fatigue started creeping in, the type of weariness that goes deep into the bone, pulling my thoughts down with it. As my steps grew shorter and shorter, the finish line seemed farther and farther away. All I could think about was this torturous task. I started getting passed by others, causing doubt to enter my thoughts. I hurt so much I began thinking there was no way I could continue. I wanted this award and all I needed was to finish this final test and it would be mine, so I pushed on. I focused my thoughts on reaching the end and as it got closer, I started worrying about finishing on time. This caused an overwhelming feeling of panic and a much-needed burst of adrenaline. With this newfound energy came resolve, and I would take off, intent on running the rest of the way. After jogging a short distance, reality would hit as my body rejected this command to run and I resumed my dead-man shuffle.

I became so focused inward and consumed with these struggles that I lost track of my buddies. This became my own battle and all I cared about was getting to the end. I was too proud to quit so I kept pushing on. Panic, jog, shuffle. Panic, jog, shuffle. An endless cycle that totally consumed me.

I continued this slow march forward when I noticed that the guys passing me were moving just a little bit faster and with more purpose. Heads were lifted, looking ahead instead of down at their feet. This was contagious, giving me energy that I didn't know I had, and my pace began to pick up. I started hearing voices cheering in the distance and realized it was almost over. With one last surge of energy, I crossed the finish line before collapsing on the side of the road. It was over and I finished in time.

I lay there in the shade, oblivious to everything, for only a few minutes until someone hollered at me to get up and walk it off before my muscles started cramping. I got up as told, even though I felt like I had already walked everything completely off in the past three hours. I slowly made my way towards the barracks for a long, hot shower. The shower refreshed my mind but my entire body still felt like I had been hit by a bus. I slowly dressed and made my way to the chow hall for a much-needed meal before the award ceremony and trip back to the Rock.

Because of the high standards and difficulty for the German Armed Forces Badge, there were many soldiers who didn't qualify. It was designed to reward excellence after all. I successfully completed the testing with a bronze qualification, and was presented with the award in a ceremony that evening. It was an honor to receive this award and I proudly wore on my dress uniform for the duration of my career.

Chapter 9
Grafenwoehr and Hohenfels

Grafenwoehr (Graf) was a training area with firing ranges for nearly every direct and indirect weapon system used by the army. Graf was the primary training grounds for units stationed in Germany and I deployed there a couple times a year for extended training sessions. Direct fire weapons, like the pistols, rifles, and machine guns, are used when the target can be seen and the fired round takes a straight path to the target. I spent most of my time at these ranges, familiarizing and firing a variety of infantry weapons. I spent a lot of time getting better with my assigned weapon, the M16 rifle, at a variety of ranges that simulated different combat situations for firing at enemy targets. For example, one range had popup targets at different distances that I shot at from a stationery position, while another range required me to advance towards the targets by running and crawling to different positions before firing.

Indirect fire weapons were typically used from greater distances, usually out of direct sight of the target. Because of this distance, the weapons are aimed high, more skyward, causing the rounds to travel in an arced trajectory towards the target. Indirect fire weapons range in size from the smaller, short range mortars to the larger howitzers that were positioned miles from the target. Indirect fire weapons require a spotter to call out firing instructions and adjustments to hit the targets.

The first thing I would do when arriving at Graf was help unload my vehicle from the train. Another smaller group was assigned to unload the containers of weapons and gear onto supply trucks. We then formed a line with our vehicles and convoyed to the area known as tent city where I would live for the next few weeks. Tent city was just that, rows of concrete slabs that large tents were erected on. Each unit was assigned specific tents and my platoon shared a tent with the mortar platoon. I got to sleep on a cot, which felt like I was staying in a luxury hotel compared to the ground I usually endured during other deployments. The vehicles were parked in a makeshift motor pool nearby.

The food on these deployments was a combination of hot meals and cold C-rations. The hot meals were pretty good and I looked forward to them. But then again, anything was better than the C-rations I had to eat once, sometimes twice, a day. I think these things had been around since World War II; at least they tasted like it. They came in cardboard boxes, each with four olive drab cans of various sizes.

Each meal included a different entrée of such delectable dishes as turkey, pork, or beef loaf that smelled like dog food (and tasted like it too). It can't be healthy to eat something that can be shaken out of the can it comes in and still retain the shape of the can.

When the C-rations were distributed, I always prayed for anything that didn't contain the word loaf in its name. My preferred choices were spaghetti, beans with wieners, and beans with meatballs.

The second can had either piece of hard chocolate in it or crackers. The third can came with peanut butter, cheese spread, or jelly. The last can in the meal had a different type of dessert item, either fruit slices or a cake such as pound, chocolate or the always popular fruit cake for dessert. I always wondered who the genius was that thought putting canned fruit cake in C-rations was a good idea. Then again, it never goes bad, but really? I don't ever recall seeing anyone eat the fruit cake. I was tempted to use it for Christmas gifts but I like my family.

One thing I learned right away was to always pack Cheese Wiz and Tobasco Sauce. Anything can be stomached with a little Cheese Wiz and Tobasco Sauce. The thing about C-rations was that they always made me look forward to the hot meals, even if the eggs were green and the gravy was called S.O.S. (which stood for "poo" on a shingle.) We trained hard so they made sure we were fed three meals a day.

As an infantry soldier, I had to be knowledgeable and proficient with a variety of weapons, so my time at Graf was spent firing these weapons. For example, in my squad one of the four of us was required to have a grenade launcher mounted on his M16 rifle and another person had to carry the M60 machine gun.

I was in a front-line unit and would have to confront the Soviets directly on the battlefield so there was a strong likelihood that I could find myself in a situation where I needed to use the weapons of fallen Soviet soldiers. The army had a supply of Soviet weapons at Graf and time was set aside to fire these weapons as well. I got to fire the Russian AK-47 rifle, their machine gun, and their rocket launcher-an important experience and a pretty cool one to.

There were three different classes of anti-armor weapons used by my unit and Graf had ranges for all of them. The most common of these was the light anti-armor weapon (LAW). This is a lightweight, tubular shaped, short range missile that was placed on the shoulder to fire at smaller vehicles. The LAW was part of every infantry squad's combat issue so I had to spend time firing this. Another shoulder-fired weapon found in every infantry squad was the Dragon, a medium weight anti-armor weapon (MAW). In my combat support company, the scout platoon carried this. The third class was the heavy anti-armor weapons which included the TOW missiles that I was trained to fire. The missiles were too expensive for everyone in my platoon to be able to fire so I spent time at ranges designed to allow us to practice targeting and tracking. At the end of the deployment to Graf, there was a final live-fire exercise and each squad in my platoon got to fire one live missile from their ITV. I was the assigned gunner in my squad so I would once again have this honor bestowed upon me. It was at this range that the air support units in my division would practice firing their weapons and dropping bombs on targets.

Once I finished with weapons training, I had to prepare for the more important live-fire exercise to close out the Grafenwoehr deployment. Everything I did was always focused on my role in the General Defense Plan to prepare me for a Soviet invasion across the border into Germany. This live fire exercise was no different and was planned like a real battle scenario from my division's assigned border positions. The largest firing range at Graf was set up specifically for this exercise with a target area and impact zone that consisted of old, discarded military vehicles to be engaged.

A battle plan was drawn up that duplicated the GDP mission for each unit, including firing orders for engaging the enemy targets. I was assigned a defensive position and a target area similar to my border responsibility with the main objective of keeping an imaginary Soviet army from advancing beyond that point. This exercise was a valuable experience since I got to see firsthand how each individual responsibility fit into the overall mission.

The live fire exercise went something like this: the infantry soldiers and scouts were on the ground nearest to the targets and they fired first. They would then retreat to their armored vehicles while Apache helicopters hovered, providing suppressive fire to cover their pullback. Once clear, the mortars would begin an assault on the targets and the anti-tank platoons fired the TOW missiles at their assigned targets. Howitzer rounds would begin landing on the targets and finally A10 planes would fly over and drop 500 pound bombs onto them. It was an impressive display of firepower to witness.

The cool thing about this training event wasn't just seeing all kinds of explosions. It also gave me the opportunity to participate in a live-fire exercise with my entire unit and see firsthand what a combat scenario on the border could look like. The use of live munitions brought a realism to this that showed me the seriousness of my responsibilities. A secondary benefit, and just as important, was it allowed me to see and experience all the elements of my unit in action and how everything fit into the GDP mission. Watching all the firepower involved in supporting my mission certainly instilled confidence in me.

I spent many days rehearsing for this live-fire exercise, and as the time neared, the pressure built. This wasn't anything like the firing ranges for personal weapons where I could fire bullet after bullet. There was a lot of money being spent on this and I didn't want to be the guy who missed his target, especially with the more specialized TOW missile. Since the exercise involved elements of the entire division, there would be a ton of eyes on it from all levels of my upper chain of command, all the way up to the division leaders. That's a whole bunch of lieutenant colonels and generals gathered on one firing range to watch this live fire scenario. Add to this all the upper echelon commanders from the European command to officials from the Pentagon who were there to watch this exercise. As the gunner on my ITV, I was aware of all the pressure we were under. It felt like an eternity from the time I pressed the trigger until he missile finally impacted the target. Time seemed to stop while I waited for confirmation of a hit or miss. I still remember the silence in the vehicle and the explosion of elation that erupted from everyone when the confirmation of a hit was announced.

At the end of the live fire exercise, preparations began for the mechanized convoy to Hohenfels. All my personal gear and equipment had to be loaded and tightly secured onto my vehicle. I would be traveling on German roads in an armored vehicle, which was no easy task. Instead of tires, on both sides of the vehicle was a track system that was turned by a huge sprocket. It had a gas pedal for acceleration and was steered with two long levers that controlled the track on each side. Braking was done by pulling both levers back at the same time. Turning required pulling the lever on the side of the desired turn, which slowed the track on that side down. To make sharp turns, one lever was pulled back hard, locking that track in place while giving it gas to move the other track, and it would turn on a dime. Sounds simple enough, but on hard surfaces like roads, the vehicle never went perfectly straight and the faster it went the less pressure it took on a lever to move it right or left. At high speeds the driver had to be totally focused, constantly making light adjustment pulls on one lever and then the other to keep it moving straight and within the right side of the road. While doing all of this, the vehicle had to maintain the designated speed and the required distance from the vehicle in front.

The ITV could go up to forty miles per hour, even faster downhill, and it was a terrifying experience for everyone at those speeds. A safe speed limit was always set for these convoys but it was impossible to maintain. Navigating up and down hills, around turns, resulted in this big yo-yo effect. This meant the drivers had no choice but to floor it most of the time to catch up. Convoying on German roads was so stressful that driving was sometimes rotated among squad members, giving me the chance to drive many times, including on my first trek to Hohenfels. My time driving was one of the most terrifying experiences I have ever had. The entire time felt like I was riding on the edge of a cliff and the slightest mistake would send me over the edge.

Armored vehicle movements inside Hohenfels is something else I will never forget. Hohenfels was a huge base specifically designed for mechanized training in an environment similar to Germany's natural terrain. The only exception was that most of the roads were not paved. This wouldn't seem so bad except these roads had been used by armored vehicles for decades. That's years and years of heavy, armored vehicles traveling back and forth over the same dirt roads. This caused the dirt to be as fine as powder and the roads like riverbeds of this dust as much as a foot deep in places. While driving on them, the air would fill with a heavy cloud of dust and cover everything. I had to wear a scarf, bandana, or a mask over my mouth and nose to keep my lungs from filling with it and goggles to protect my eyes.

The dust was mostly an inconvenience until it rained, making the roads very slippery and difficult to travel on. The mud was like cake batter and would fill the sprockets causing the vehicle to throw a track. Reconnecting a track was a difficult task under normal circumstances, so the last thing I wanted to do was reconnect it in the mud. I had to do this once and by the time the track was repaired I was covered from head to foot in muck. I saw many vehicles throw a track and need to be pulled out of the mud before repairs could be made. Fortunately, most training at Hohenfels was done off road and this situation could be avoided.

Unlike Graf, there was no tent city with cots. I was here to practice maneuvers and combat scenarios so I had to sleep whenever and wherever I could. I wasn't allowed to sleep in my vehicle so I usually just threw my sleeping bag down on the ground when it was time to sleep. If it rained, I would take the time to build a little shelter with my poncho before plopping down. I had a hammock that I used if there was time to set it up and the situation would allow it. Comfort was not a luxury in the infantry so I had to find it in little things like hammocks, Cheese Wiz, and Tabasco Sauce.

I was in a heavy armor unit so my vehicle was an equally important part of my job. All the individual training I went through was put to practical use at Hohenfels where it was integrated into the proper techniques of mechanized combat movements. To be successful moving in a combat situation, I needed to know how to use the terrain around me to my advantage for camouflage and stealth. For example, if I drove or walked along the top of the hill, it created a silhouette that could be seen from all directions. To avoid this, I was taught to always travel far enough below the top, using the hill as a backdrop, making it more difficult to see me. Just as important, I needed to be able to move in the larger components as a platoon and company when we mobilized as a battalion.

At the platoon level, I practiced traveling in a wedge formation through hilly terrain while keeping my vehicle below the tops of the hills. I spent time maneuvering along wood lines; using the trees to help camouflage my vehicles movement. Then there were the exercises of duck-and-cover movements where one vehicle would be in a cover position, weapons up, while another vehicle moved to its next covered position. I had to train extensively in these different formations and movements to know the best methods to use under various conditions and terrains.

Defensive exercises were practiced where I would move into an area and prepare a position to defend against an attack. My vehicle had to be camouflaged, security put in place, and fire zone maps drawn for my assigned sector to engage. And, of course, I had to practice my targeting responsibilities for acquiring a target and the firing procedures to engage it.

Every deployment included chemical and biological training, and I spent most of my time at Hohenfels in my protective gear. The threat of a chemical or biological attack was always a very real possibility so I had to wear my suit most of the time. This always made me very hot and miserable and created some pretty nasty aromas inside the vehicle. As I went through these training exercises, orders would be given to move up and down the different threat levels from MOPP 1 to MOPP 4. By the end of my time at Hohenfels I felt like a zombie.

When the end of training did finally come, I had to prepare the vehicle for the return to the Rock. This meant a long session at the wash rack to remove as much of the dried muck as I could. The dust was so fine it found its way into every nook and cranny and was very difficult to wash off. Fortunately, I didn't have to worry about thoroughly cleaning it until I got back to base where it would have to be pressure washed to get it clean enough for the white glove inspection. Here, I just had to get the worst of the dirt before loading it onto the train flatbeds.

It was always a relief when I finally boarded the train for the ride back to the Rock. The Grafenwoehr/Hohenfels training was the longest deployment I did each year and I was exhausted by the end of it. We all were. Before the train would depart, the sound of snoring was all that could be heard, and mine was the loudest.

I still had the grueling recovery and inspections to endure but that was only a distant concern at that moment. As the train sped through the beautiful German countryside, I enjoyed this reprieve and slept like a baby.

Chapter 10
The Fulda Gap

The mission for all units stationed in West Germany during the Cold War was to mobilize quickly and deploy to the eastern border to take up defensive positions if the Soviets attacked. All of this was laid out in the General Defense Plan (GDP). Each unit in the 3rd Armored Division had a specific area of the Fulda Gap that they were responsible to defend. Upon arriving there, I would move into my predetermined defensive position with only one objective, to defend and hold the gap until the main forces in Europe could arrive. This was the reason troops were stationed in Germany and why I had to go through such rigorous training every day, to be prepared for this mission. Yet the full impact of my responsibilities never really hit me until my battalion actually deployed to this location.

When I arrived at the German base near my border assignment, it was surreal. For the first time, I began to feel the full weight of my responsibilities as I realized where I was and what could happen there. The reason for this deployment was to allow us to see up close the area we might one day defend. It also gave us a chance to meet and train with our German counterparts who were permanently stationed there to monitor and patrol this portion of the Fulda Gap.

My nights were spent sleeping in barracks- a nice change of pace for a deployment. One morning I went to the exact location I would be required to defend. The Cold War was so sensitive at that time that I had to ride a truck there because bringing armored vehicles might have been seen as an aggressive move and trigger a reaction from the Soviets.

When I got there, I was allowed to roam the area to familiarize myself with the terrain. My mood was somber and my thoughts were preoccupied so I didn't really notice the beautiful, scenic mountains and steep ravines around me full of trees as far as the eye could see. My gaze moved towards the direction of Czechoslovakia and the realization of everything hit me. If the Soviets invaded, this is where it would happen. This is where I could die. I noticed how quiet it was and knew everyone else was having similar thoughts. I found myself speaking in a hushed voice, like I was afraid the Soviets would hear and start shooting at me.

The GDP mission required me to prevent the Soviet and Warsaw Pact forces from advancing through this area of the gap for forty-eight hours to allow the NATO main forces to arrive. Considering the size of the military they would be sending across this border, few of us in these front line positions would survive. This was a responsibility shared by everyone who was ever stationed in Germany during the Cold War. Knowing this didn't change anything, so I didn't dwell on it.

My squad was assigned the task of finding a defensive position for our vehicle that would provide the best cover and camouflage. As the gunner, I was shown my assigned target area and had to draw up a map of it showing as much detail as possible. The seriousness of my responsibilities continued to weigh heavily on me as I completed this assignment. I spent about half a day getting familiar with my target area before returning to the barracks.

Towards the end of the deployment, I could go to the club on post. I was here for training so all I had to wear were my fatigues. The club was packed with German and American soldiers in uniform like me so I didn't feel out of place. There was one American soldier, an E-4 specialist, who stood out because he was wearing his dress uniform. He was supposed to transfer stateside to out-process from the army while we were deployed but had gotten into trouble back at the Rock. Trouble that had involved an officer's wife. The MP's had to escort him to this post to be given an Article-15 by the battalion commander before releasing him to finish transferring stateside. An Article-15 is the highest form of punishment a commander is authorized to give on his own. The next level of punishment would be to initiate court martial proceedings which takes the judicial matter out of the commander's control. The commander has all sorts of punishment options available under an article-15. The proceedings for this guy had happened earlier in the day which was why he wasn't still in the custody of the MP's and was sitting at my table drinking with me. The commander had stripped him of his rank of an E-5 sergeant, moving him down one pay grade to an E-4 specialist, and was sending him back the next day.

A small group of us pulled tables together and started some heavy beer drinking. It didn't take long before everyone was laughing loudly and singing raunchy songs, drawing the attention of everyone in the bar. For some reason, someone started singing the Mickey Mouse Club song, which quickly led to the creation of a more colorful version that would become like a drunken anthem to us for many months to come. The "F" bomb was substituted for Mickey and "a-g-a-i-n" for "m-o-u-s-e" with creative phrases in place of the other lyrics. After the lines "F'ed Again", the table was pounded twice. Eventually, the whole bar of German and American soldiers was singing along and pounding the table at the appropriate time. It was so awesome! It was pretty cool that German soldiers had joined in, but what really made it special was that everyone in the bar was singing. Not just guys from my company, but guys from the whole battalion. Our singing this ridiculous song had changed the whole atmosphere, turning this small military bar with its small private conversations into *Cheers* for one night, *where everybody knows your name*.

After quite a bit of beer, loud singing, and even louder laughing, the club announced it was closing. Bars always have a way of closing before you want them to. One German soldier who had joined our table, invited everyone to come to his house to drink some more. I wasn't ready to quit drinking yet so I didn't hesitate to accept this offer. There were only a few others like me, stupid enough to take him up on this offer and sneak off post. It was no surprise the guy who just lost his rank from the article-15 was in this group, dress uniform and all.

When I arrived at his house, it was obvious that his wife wasn't very happy with him for bringing a bunch of drunk Americans home in the middle of the night. He was just as drunk so he was oblivious to her irritation. As we sat in his living room, drinking and laughing, he eventually noticed his wife's not-so-discrete glares. In his current state, he was clueless to her anger and he did what any guy would do in this situation- he asked her what was wrong. I didn't need to speak German to know he was really in the doghouse now for this escapade. Once she was finished chewing him out, she took his keys from him and made him tell us it was time to go. This was a smart decision because he was in no condition to drive anyway. Feeling awkward now, I quickly made my way to the door and went outside. I wasn't in any condition to walk, but with no other options, off I went.

Now I had a real problem. How on earth was I going to get back onto a secured German post? As we walked back towards base, we began to formulate a plan. Turns out that having a recently demoted sergeant in his dress uniform sneak off base with us was a blessing. We decided to make it look like he had caught us off post and was marching us back to our unit. To add even more authenticity to our ploy, he started calling out cadence as the gate came into view, "One, two, three, four, left, right, left." Imagine a handful of scared, inebriated guys trying to stay in single file formation while marching in step through the front gate of a foreign country's military base. I was terrified I would get caught and end up getting an Article 15 as well.

But it worked! It worked so well the security guards stood at attention and saluted as we passed through. I couldn't believe it. As soon as I was out of sight, I busted out laughing before sprinting off towards my barracks and sneaking inside. I quickly made my way to my bed, snickering the whole way.

Like any great adventure that involves rule bending and alcohol, it could never be shared because of the fear of being punished. None of us wanted to be the guy in his dress uniform next time.

Chapter 11
Reforger
Return of Forces to Germany

When World War II ended, Europe was left in a very fragile condition. Europeans had just survived a war that saw their countries defeated and taken over by Hitler and his Nazi regime. The whole continent was in shambles from the brutality of the war that finally defeated him. To make matter worse, Hitler had attacked the east and brought Stalin and the USSR into the war. Fighting a two-front war may have played a big part in Hitler's fall, but in his zeal, he had succeeded in putting the Soviets, and communism, on the winning side of the war.

The end of the war saw Germany split into two separate countries, east and west, and divided into four zones to be governed by the four occupying countries at the end of the war. Since the Soviet Union was one of these countries, it was given the newly formed East Germany to govern, allowing this European country to fall under the control of the Soviet Union and communism.

European leaders were afraid that when the US soldiers left, the Soviets would take advantage of their weakened condition and invade. West Germany, the logical point of an invasion, was demilitarized as part of the conditions ending the war so there was nothing to stop the overwhelming size of the Soviet military from steamrolling through and conquering the rest of Europe, just like Hitler had done.

To help prevent this from happening and to reassure the European countries that we wouldn't abandon them, the United States agreed to leave a sizeable military force stationed throughout West Germany. The General Defense Plan was then drawn up to stop any such invasion. Return of forces to Germany (Reforger) was established as an annual exercise to allow military units from the US and its allies to train together in preparation for a possible Soviet invasion.

Reforger was a tool used during the Cold War that served several purposes. It was held in West Germany so our forces could conduct combat exercises in a mock war situation in the country the GDP mission required to be defended. Indirectly, it reassured our allies that we still had their backs if the Soviets made a move, and acted as a show of force to discourage any soviet attempt of expanding communism into Europe.

Units in Germany alternated years that they participated in Reforger but I was fortunate and got to participate both years I was there. The first year I was part of the orange forces and the second year I got to experience it from the view point of an evaluator. Both were unique experiences that afforded me the opportunity to see this exercise from different perspectives.

Reforger was a war game so it needed to mimic combat scenarios. To be realistic, sides were designated as orange and blue forces. Not much different than when kids played war games in their back yard and nobody wanted to be the bad guy.

In 1981, technology in the military was pretty primitive compared to now. My unit may have just gotten new armored vehicles but all the fancy high tech equipment our military now employs was only found in science fiction books and movies back then.

So how do you tell the difference between orange units and blue units? This is where the top-notch military technology comes in. Every vehicle had square signs painted either orange or blue with numbers stenciled on them. Using rope, these signs were hung on the four sides of the vehicles. If a vehicle was spotted and engaged by the opposing side, the grid coordinates, type of vehicle, and number on the sign had to be called in over the radio. This would be relayed to the vehicle on its radio frequency and the crew had to immediately stop where they were and raise their engine panel to signal being out of action. The vehicle and crew would remain there until cleared to rejoin their unit for the next combat scenario. Those simple colored signs gave us a way to add realism to these war games. Looking through the sights on my vehicle, I could easily distinguish who the enemy was and read the number on the sign. I would yell out the number and while my squad leader radioed it in for the kill, I would be scanning for the next enemy target.

The cool part of Reforger was it allowed units to perform combat training within the rural and urban areas of West Germany. A battle with the Soviets wasn't going to take place on a training post like Hohenfels, and Reforger gave me the experience of actually defending and fighting an opposing force in a civilized area. The various battle scenarios required one side to defend an area while the other side acted as the aggressor by advancing to take the area.

Plans would be drawn up by top commanders at the division level and passed down to the brigade commanders, working their way down the chain of command for unit commanders to implement. There would be brigade-level meetings where the battalion commanders would be given their missions and plans would be developed for the implementation of them. This was followed by battalion meetings to establish company responsibilities. Company commanders then held their own briefings with platoon leaders, outlining what the company mission was and they put together a plan for each platoon. And lastly, the platoon leaders outlined the mission to their platoon sergeants and then met with section and squad leaders so they could prepare us, the grunts, for the upcoming battle.

The defenders would move into the designated battle area and set up their defensive positions. At a predetermined time, the other side would begin their advance to try and secure the area. When an opposing target was engaged, it was called in over the radio. Each unit had several controllers assigned to them who monitored the "battles" on the radio and travelled with them. They trailed units in jeeps, trying to remain out of sight while they refereed the exercise. When the controller heard the hit called in on the radio, he confirmed the vehicle was pulled out of the exercise until the battle was over. Controllers tagged along on foot with infantry ground units who could assault an armored vehicle and take it out with their anti-armor weapons or call it in for indirect fire hit.

This was a pretty simple system that, oddly enough, worked extremely well. The reason it worked is because soldiers have integrity and honor. Cheating wasn't part of our make-up and would never even have been considered. These values were ingrained into me every day starting from the moment I stepped off the bus at Fort Benning. I was proud to serve my country and I took my responsibilities seriously. Cheating was not the honorable thing to do and every guy around me felt the same way, including the guys across the field with a different color on their vehicle. I knew they were just as honorable. This is why the colored board system, primitive as it seemed, worked.

As the battle continued, the defenders would eventually have to withdraw. Using the German terrain, buildings, barns, and whatever else was available to cover the retreat, each unit would withdraw and give up the ground it had just defended. The unit on the offensive would be advancing, using the same cover tactics to secure this land, before beginning another advance until encountering the defenders in a new area.

The order would eventually come down ending the day's exercise and units would move to a designated area for the night to set up a secure camp and regroup for the next day. Security details were set in place with shifts assigned to every soldier in the unit. Maintenance of equipment, weapon systems, and vehicles was done to insure readiness for the next day while the leaders gathered to go over every detail of that day's battles. While this was happening, commanders at the top of the chain of command were putting together plans for the next day. When they were complete, meetings were conducted to pass along assignments for each unit. Briefings were then held down the chain of command, ending at the platoon level, to delegate new responsibilities for the next day. By morning, every soldier would know of that day's mission and it began all over again.

One thing about deploying for training I already knew was I wouldn't be getting much sleep. There is no real way to create the actual stress of being in a combat situation. My body needed to learn how to let my brain instinctively guide my movements and control how I reacted under duress. Just like in basic training, sleep deprivation was the best tool for this. If my body was extremely fatigued or under stress, I needed my movements and reactions to be automatic or second nature. Whenever I deployed, sleep became something I learned to do without.

Reforger was no different; in fact, I got even less sleep during this. Between briefings, chow, maintenance procedures, and the hundreds of other responsibilities I had, sleep was at the bottom of the list. When I did get permission to sleep, I had guard duty responsibilities. Guard duty schedules were usually platoon-wide in a camp. If I were in a combat situation at night, then I would have to do this by crew, which meant rotating shifts between the four of us. If I were lucky, I got the first shift because it was hard to wake up after an hour or two of sleep when I was exhausted.

At the beginning of Reforger, the entire German countryside could be used for maneuvering between positions. I was briefed prior to the exercise to be careful and avoid damaging any property. Serious damage was avoided, especially when traveling through the cities, towns, and busy roads. But on farmland, and property outside the cities, there was more freedom allowed for movements. Since most of the combat movements and battles were in fields and wooded areas, we could stay away from buildings and high-dollar damage.

No amount of caution can eliminate damage completely with an exercise this large. The budget each year for Reforger included reimbursement to any German citizen whose property was damaged during the exercise. There were auditors in the field followed the battle scenarios and documented the damage as it occurred. It was a running joke among us that some Germans encouraged armored vehicles to cut through their crops for the big payday they would get from Uncle Sam. If the military was really paying $500 for toilet seats, imagine what was paid for damaged corn.

There occasionally was more serious damage that happened with so many tanks and armored personnel carriers involved. I recall seeing the damage in one small town that happened when a tank gunner didn't get the turret moved in sync with the tank as it made a turn. This caused the barrel of the gun to clip a building on the corner and take out a two-foot section of it. Another time I saw where a tank had rolled downhill, through a vineyard, and into a home. The unit had taken up position on a steep hillside and the soldiers hadn't properly blocked the tank's track. Fortunately, I don't recall any serious injuries during Reforger either year.

At some point near the end of Reforger, the damage assessments would reach a specific level. Once this happened, restrictions would be put in place requiring vehicles to remain on roads for the remaining days of the exercise.

One of the unofficial perks of Reforger was something unauthorized, but still enjoyed by most. Every German town seemed to have bakeries with fresh breads, butcher shops with cold cuts, and small grocery stores. During down moments between battles, there were many "clandestine" supply runs into town. There was always someone willing to make one of these runs, platoon leaders, platoon sergeants or one of us. C-Rations were always nasty, and eventually even the hot field chow got old, so orders were put together, money collected and away they would go.

Reforger was a blast in some aspects. As a kid, I had a GI Joe doll with the kung-fu grip and little plastic army guys I would spread across my bedroom floor. I played army, cowboys and Indians, and tied a towel around my neck to become Superman, running around my neighborhood and my backyard doing battle with countless imaginary bad guys. Boys will always be boys, even as adults, and Reforger was like a big playground but with an actual enemy to do battle against. It didn't matter that the enemy wasn't real but guys just like me with a different-colored number on their vehicle. This was just like those days growing up with my brothers and friends - armed with a cowboy holster and cap guns, a bow made from a stick and string, pine cone grenades, I made pretend machine gun sounds as I fought like the world depended on it. My imagination would take over until victory was mine.

Reforger was like that. The weapons and armored vehicles were real but I still had to pretend I was firing live rounds. I knew the seriousness of the exercise and losing was not an option. I knew if I got killed it wasn't real, I would then have to answer to my chain of command for dying, and nobody likes getting berated for failure. But just like those childhood battles, I wanted to be the one standing on the hill at the end of the war, whooping and hollering about my victory. So, I went through these exercises, with training controlling my actions and movements, and letting my imagination fill in the rest.

About halfway through my time in Germany, the company commander reassigned me to be his driver. In the fall of 1982 the leadership in my unit was assigned as controllers for that year's Reforger, giving me the chance to experience this huge training exercise from a different perspective. The controllers had to arrive a few days in advance of the participating units to attend briefings. This gave me the opportunity to be present for the arrival of the air assault units when they parachuted in to kick off the exercise. I managed to park my jeep near the drop zone and had an excellent view of the row of C-130 planes when they approached. I watched in awe as an endless stream of parachutes appeared behind each plane, descending in a diagonal line towards the horizon. The entire sky seemed to instantly fill up with parachutes drifting slowly towards the ground in front of me. Minutes later, another line of planes would appear and before I knew it, the sky was filled again.

Once the last of the paratroopers had safely landed and disappeared into the woods, another row of planes could be seen approaching. Before long the sky was filled with much larger parachutes as vehicles and equipment were being dropped. I watched breathlessly as each piece descended slowly, landing perfectly in the open field in front of me and quickly retrieved by the recently landed paratroopers. Before I knew it, it was over. When I looked around, there was hardly any sign of what I had just witnessed. I still get goose bumps remembering the sight of this extraordinary landing I was fortunate to see. The precision that these elite units utilize as they drop equipment and troops into a combat environment is an amazing thing to witness. This was one of many little "perks" I got being the commander's driver.

I was fortunate that CPT Kranepuhl had taken a liking to me and treated me more as a friend than a subordinate, becoming a mentor to me. As a company commander, he had to participate in the battalion - and -company level briefings with the unit we were assigned to. This gave me access to copies of the maps and battle plans for the upcoming battles each day. After each briefing, he would go over every-thing again with me, every little detail, until I understood it. He taught me how to read the terrain on a map and how it was used in de-vising the strategies for the upcoming battles. He showed me how this was used to construct the map overlays used in the combat brief-ings. I learned about the different tactics being used and the pros and cons of them. He seemed to enjoy teaching me and always encour-aged me to ask questions. Unlike the controllers assigned to platoons and squads, we had the freedom to roam and choose where to be as long as we followed our assigned company. It wasn't unusual for him to hand me the maps after one of these sessions and have us reverse roles. He would become the driver and I would have to navigate as we made our way around the countryside to oversee the different platoons in the company we were officiating.

When he wasn't teaching me, I had to study these maps and know the general lay of the land so that I could quickly go to a loca-tion when he directed. It was not unusual to be driving down a road, have him spot armored vehicles somewhere and shout, "Hard right and fast." I would immediately make a sharp right turn into a field and hit the gas. On one occasion, there was disastrous consequences for speeding through a field. More stupidity on my part than anything.

Chewing tobacco was very popular among soldiers in Germa-ny. I am a nonsmoker but had been enticed into trying Skoal during my first deployment to Hohenfels to help me stay awake those short nights with guard duty shifts. Surprisingly, most the nonsmokers in my unit chewed tobacco. I started with Skoal because it was the most available in the PX. It came in a wax-coated cardboard can with an aluminum lid and didn't stay fresh long, so by the time it reached Germany it was already old and drying out. There was another brand available in the PX that I didn't like at all called Copenhagen that was real fine and gave me a buzz. As soon as I put a pinch in my lip, I would get flushed and lightheaded and felt like my eyes were going to pop out. The only time I chewed it was when I had to keep awake at night. I would chew tobacco for years to come and Copenhagen al-ways had this effect on me.

Smoking wasn't allowed in any military vehicles so most smokers chewed tobacco to. Chewing requires a lot of spitting and when I was in my ITV, my room, or anywhere else, I kept an empty can of Coke handy to spit in. I always carried a P38 can opener to open my C-rations and had learned how to use this to remove the top of the pop can to make a spittoon. When I became the commander's jeep driver, I had a cup holder that I hung from the defrost vent above the gear shift, so I could drink a can of pop while driving around. It wasn't as good of an idea when I decided to use it to hold my home-made spittoon, especially considering the doors of the jeep were always removed on deployments and all I had to do was turn my head left and spit. The real boneheaded part of this was that for no logical reason at all, I would always wait until it was full before emptying it. The disastrous outcome is obvious now but I honestly never thought this through when I was doing it.

It was at my second Reforger that I would learn the hard way just how bad an idea it was. I was driving down a road next to an open field when the company we were assigned to announced enemy contact over the radio. CPT Kranepuhl called out for a hard-right turn which I made without incident. I floored it and as I was working my way through the gears, I hit a hole and suddenly realized the disgusting consequences of not thinking this through. I spent the rest of the day with a nasty brown stain on my lap. I'm not sure what CPT Kranepuhl's reaction was. I was so embarrassed I continued driving like nothing happened.

All throughout this Reforger, I got to see the planning done at the battalion level and watch it as it was implemented all the way down to the platoons in the company we followed. I saw how commanders utilized support units into their front-line battle plans. I got to watch from a distance as units on the offense moved in on defensive positions and how defenders reacted and then withdrew into backup positions. Captain Kranepul always explained the everything to me as they unfolded.

I would see the army with a different perspective at the end of this Reforger exercise. No longer were the mundane drills just training to be endured nor was the torturous physical training senseless. I had a peek behind the curtain and got a glimpse of the bigger picture. I began to see and understand how my job responsibilities fit into the bigger picture. From this point on, I would pay more attention to detail and start taking more of a lead during training. I didn't know it at the time, but the seed planted here would have more of an effect transforming me than basic training ever did.

All the successes in my military career can be traced back to Reforger 1982 and CPT Kranepuhl.

Chapter 12
Short Timer

It's quite ironic now, looking back and realizing how much I enjoyed my two years in Germany. The physical demands were so overwhelming that none of us could wait to leave. Time has a way of softening hardships and I suspect that most of the people who served there during the Cold War now look back with fond memories as well. Being stationed in West Germany during a time of such high tension between the east and west, there was always a strong possibility of war, and I had to be ready. That's why I was there. I had to train hard and remain vigilant to keep prepared to be successful if this threats did arise. There weren't any days that could be considered a normal or average day for me, there couldn't be, at least not in the combat arms units.

I deployed all the time. It might occasionally be for just a few days out the back gate, but usually it was for one or two weeks, with the longest deployment being a month. My time was spent preparing for a deployment, training, and returning to the Rock. Then came the recovery process of cleaning and maintaining my vehicle and equipment, followed by the ever-so-popular inspections of everything. I'd get a couple of three-and-four day weekends after the final inspections and then start this cycle over again. When I was off duty, I took full advantage of this time, drinking and enjoying life as only a young man in a foreign country could. We all did. I trained hard and when I wasn't training I partied just as hard. There was nothing else, just this continuous cycle of training and partying.

Prostitution was legal in Germany and a short train ride to Frankfurt was all it took to get to the largest red light district in the country. Within walking distance of the train station, and about a block removed from the main road, was building after building of these women. They were nothing like the brothels and whorehouses portrayed on television or in books. Every building had one entrance with a single hallway that wound through five or six floors of small, private rooms consisting of nothing more than a bed and a bathroom. When a girl was working, she would sit in front of her door and solicit customers as they walked by. The rooms they rented must have been assigned based upon how much money they made so that the high earners would be rewarded with the better paying rooms on the lower floors, closer to the entrance. This had to be true because the rooms higher up and further away from the entrance always had the uglier the girls in them. The rooms on the top floors were scary. There were dozens of these buildings within a couple of blocks.

The main road that led from the train station to the red-light district was lined with stage shows, strippers, and peepshows, down both sides of this street. The clubs with stage shows charged a cover price to get in plus a two-drink minimum of their overpriced drinks. There were pretty, scantily dressed women working for these clubs, enticing customers to buy them overpriced, watered down drinks, just like the bar I encountered at Fort Benning. The difference was that these women were also high-priced prostitutes soliciting guys into private rooms behind the bar. Surprisingly, I don't think any of these adult venues was the most popular destination for soldiers in the red-light district. Nope, I think the biggest draw was the McDonald's located right in the middle of all of this. The place was always packed with American soldiers every time I ate there. The fact that they served beer didn't hurt either.

I didn't travel to Frankfurt very often. I usually only went there when I was homesick and wanted to call home. I could call collect from several places but if I went to the train station in Frankfurt, I could make the phone call and pay for it myself. It was a simple set up with three or four private phone rooms and an operator who placed my call. When I was done, she would calculate the charge and I paid her. Otherwise, I didn't need to go there to party. Most of us preferred to drink in the barracks and there were clubs closer to the Rock if I wanted to get out.

I spent most of my time with the maintenance guys my last year. It seemed like we were together every moment of every day. Mike Arthur was my closest friend and we were inseparable when we were off duty. When we decided to party away from the Rock, Scotty Edwards, and Bear (SGT Bear) were usually with us.

There's a small town just a short cab ride from the Rock called Wetzlar that was my destination of choice if I wanted to hang out in a bar. The Mini Sound was like any small-town bar with wall-to-wall booths and tables and a small DJ booth in the main room. MTV had just been introduced making rock videos popular. In the corner, next to the DJ, was a small TV mounted on the wall that they would play some of the new rock videos on. Roller Derby, which involved scantily clad women roller skating around an oval track, fighting and body slamming each other into the walls was also popular back then. The bar liked to show clips of this while blasting rock music in the background. It was cool to watch this while drinking with my buddies. At some point in the evening, a quarter would be laid on the table signaling the start of a drinking game. It was a pretty simple game of a bouncing a quarter on the table and trying to land it in a full glass of beer, but I wasn't very good at it. If it did land in the glass, I got to pick someone who had to chug the glass of beer without swallowing the quarter. This wasn't as easy as it sounds and if someone was really good at it, they would dominate the game. Tempers would start to flair and the game would have to be ended before punches were thrown. The bar closed at midnight, which was way too early most of the time. Once the booze started having an effect, and my blood was pumping from the videos and loud music, going back to the barracks was the last thing I wanted to do.

When the club started throwing everyone out at closing time, a huge mob of us would make the short walk uphill to another club. This one was like a Hard Rock Cafe but before I had ever heard of one. The walls were covered with rock memorabilia; motorcycle displays and leopard-printed rugs. Half the club consisted of a perimeter of booths circling a dance floor and the bar was in other half with wall to wall tables. The music was mostly hard rock and much louder, creating more of a partying atmosphere with less visiting than the last club. I usually just drank when I was there. I would venture out on the dance floor from time to time for one of the stupid audience participation things they did like the Hokey Pokey or the conga line. Every night near closing time, the club held one of the silliest of all the audience participation events, the Chicken Dance song. Every person in the bar jumped up and participated in this ridiculous song played by accordions. I am sure I looked like a fool out there, flapping my arms and making chicken beaks with my hands in unison to this absurd song. I recently heard this song being played and was shocked when I saw my granddaughters go through the same motions thirty or so years later. Go figure...

This club would eventually close and I would grab a cab back to base with my buddies. Across the street from the main gate were a couple of small businesses that catered specifically to the soldiers. The one that was frequented the most often was referred to as the "Head Shop" because of the drug paraphernalia they sold, but their popularity was mostly because of the big selection of music albums and cassette tapes they offered. They also sold tickets to the many concerts held in Germany. There was a sewing shop where my uniforms could be cleaned, altered, and have patches and ranks sewn onto them. It was the little pizza shop with a walk-up window and a couple picnic tables that I liked to visit after these long nights drinking. After closing the bars down, the cabs would drop me and my buddies off at the main gate. By this time in the evening we would be famished and grab a pizza to take back to the barracks.

I could also buy bottled German beer across from the main gate. I don't know how they kept from running out because I always saw guys on beer runs and carrying cartons of bottles across the street and through the gate. I believe Leichen was the brand brewed and sold in my area. German beer is designed to be drunk at room temperature and takes some getting used to. I refrigerated it the first few times I drank it because I thought beer was meant to be drunk cold. Not German beer. It was nasty coming out of my refrigerator so it didn't take me long to get used to drinking it at room temperature.

The breweries sold what was called Double Bach Beer around the holidays. I was told that the brewers cleaned their vats at the end of year and the Double Bach was the thicker stuff found at the bottom. I am not sure how true this was but it was certainly thicker and it packed a huge wallop. Double Bach hangovers were the worst to recover from.

I spent every waking moment with my roommates and the other guys in my unit so there were times I just wanted to do things alone. Sometimes, I would walk to the bars and restaurants in the surrounding area. It wasn't unusual at all for me to walk to the train station and take off somewhere. I might get off the train in a smaller town, find a place to eat or some obscure bar to hang out in. Most of the time, the locals in these towns were nice, but occasionally I would enter one of these bars and be told they didn't speak English. I knew this wasn't true but figured they didn't want their bar to become a hangout for American soldiers and said this to discourage me. I'd stay for a few drinks anyway. Sometimes I didn't want to be bothered either. Elvis was still very popular in Germany and I knew that every juke box had his songs if I wanted some American music. Plus, playing Elvis usually broke the ice and the patrons would at least be cordial towards me while I was there. It was during one of these solo excursions that I stumbled upon the party of all parties.

Every year the Germans hold their annual Oktoberfest, a month-long celebration. I would see these huge, white beer tents the locals would fill up every evening, and all day on weekends, popping up all over the countryside. There was always lots of beer and live music inside these tents which provided another opportunity and excuse to go drinking. Most of the guys preferred the bars in Wetzlar, so I usually ventured out on my own during Oktoberfest. I loved the German people, drinking with them in these tents, listening to their music and celebrating whatever it was they celebrated during Oktoberfest. As I have mentioned, I really enjoyed German beer back then.

I was deployed for many weekends but when I wasn't, I drank. Many weekends off, I just stayed on base and drank in my room with my roommates, or in someone else's room playing poker. There were a few weekends that I would choose not to drink, but those were rare. I also had relatives I could visit during part of my time in Germany. My cousin Pat Hensley was a Civil Engineer for the U.S. and got assigned to Frankfurt during my second year. I would go visit her when I could. I loved the few times I did this because we would play cards and laugh late into the night, having a great time without alcohol. In the morning, she would make me French toast, going through a whole loaf of bread before I couldn't eat anymore. My grandmother and Aunt Francis flew to Germany for a few weeks and stayed with Pat during my last summer there. I took a few days leave and stayed with them while they were there. Pat had this tiny car that the four of us squeezed into, touring parts of Frankfurt I had never seen before.

My cousin, Tony Cantrell, got assigned to an air force base in the western part of Germany, near the Luxemburg border. My deployments never took me to that part of the country so I looked forward to visiting him. Towards the end of my time in Germany I could get a weekend free to visit him and his wife Lori before I left. By this time, I was very comfortable traveling alone and navigating the German train system. I took a train to Frankfurt and transferred onto one heading west to Luxemburg. It was the longest train ride I had ever taken, but it was worth it. I spent a wonderful weekend with a cousin I have known my whole life. I also got to enjoy many home cooked meals. I'd almost forgotten food could taste so delicious.

All in all, my time in Germany was an endless cycle that wore me down. Every soldier counted the days until his assignment was up and he could return stateside, and I think we all kept track of this number in our heads. It wasn't acceptable to call myself a short timer until the halfway point in my assignment was passed. The countdown would become an obsession from then on because I was so anxious to get out of Germany. It was this way for everyone I knew. By the time I hit my halfway point, I knew my job very well and understood the importance of always being ready. The rigorous training, running and marching was still very physical, but I was now used to the everyday demands and it started to become more of a routine, more monotonous, and it just wore on me. I couldn't wait to get stateside where it had to be better than this. It certainly couldn't be any worse. Crossing that halfway point became significant because it meant I had fewer days ahead of me than behind. The countdown was just another way that soldiers bonded with each other, sharing this common goal and desire to get out of Germany.

There were a handful of short-timer songs that everyone knew the words to. Steve Miller Band's "Fly like an Eagle," Simon and Garfunkel's "Homeward Bound," and John Denver's "Leaving on a Jet Plane" were a few of the favorites but Merle Haggard's "Silver Wings" was the short timer's anthem and nearly choked guys up when it was played. All conversation would cease and we sang it as loud as we could, thinking of that big silver-winged plane that would one day take us home. The clubs knew the popularity of this song and frequently played it and the locals sang right along with us. Pretty cool! Whenever I was drinking in the barracks, we would end up taking turns playing each other's favorite short-timer song and we would sing each of them at the top of our lungs. When the medley of short timer songs ended, there would be hugs and high fives and the sharing and comparing of each other's short-timer countdown. We would then congratulate the guy who was the shortest, short timer in the room, while dreaming of the day we would be the one being congratulated.

As my short timer countdown shrank, and the big day got closer, I was drinking heavy every weekend night. The week before my scheduled departure, I returned from a deployment and was given a four-day weekend. That's four days off-duty leading into my long-awaited departure on the fifth day. I think I spent the entire time off celebrating with all my buddies. Captain Kranepuhl had offered to take me to the airport, so on the morning of my flight I grabbed my duffle bag and staggered down to his office. With my head pounding and a five-day growth of beard, I entered his office. He laughed at my condition and told me I had to shave before we could leave. Like a good soldier, I complied, and with no beard to add color to my face, I am sure I looked like a zombie. I know I felt like one.

He got me to the airport and I boarded my plane for that long flight home to Indiana and a long overdue leave to see my family. I thought that flight would finally put Germany behind me and I was anxious to begin my next assignment at Fort Knox, a short two-hour drive from home. Unfortunately, this transition wasn't quite as smooth as it should have been and served as proof that drinking lots of alcohol before traveling is a dumb idea. I got to my Mom's house and when I started unpacking my duffle bag the first thing I saw was a sleeping bag. *Uh Oh!* I pulled it out and noticed a steel pot and other pieces of combat gear and no sign of my stuff. This wasn't my duffle bag. I had grabbed my roommate, Scotty Edwards's by mistake and mine was probably still sitting on the floor in my old room. All my camouflage uniforms, Class A dress uniforms, dress shoes, combat boots, everything was going to need to be replaced.

I didn't even have a uniform to report to my new unit in.

Chapter 13
4th Battalion, 54th Infantry

I arrived at Fort Knox in April of 1983 and reported directly to my unit, the AT Platoon of Combat Support Company, 4th Battalion, 54th Infantry of the 194th Armored Brigade. This unit already had the ITV's so it was an easy transition for me. I was an E-4 Specialist when I arrived, which was the same rank as corporal but not a leadership position.

The atmosphere here was completely different than that in Germany. I wasn't living and training a few hours away from a communist border and the pressure of being the first line of defense was gone. This was Radcliff, Kentucky and I could drive home and see my family in just a little less time than it took to get to my GDP border position from the Rock. It may have felt different being further away from the immediate threat of a Soviet invasion, but the threat was still there.

Just as I was leaving Germany, President Reagan, never shy about his disdain for communism, had increased tensions by calling the Soviet Union an "Evil Empire." A few weeks later he would announce his Strategic Defense Initiative (SDI) which called for the development of a missile defense system for protecting the United States from a nuclear attack by using weapons that could be fired from land and satellites. Even though President Reagan insisted SDI was strictly a defensive program, the Soviets believed otherwise and saw it as a threat. This lead to increased saber rattling by the Soviets and heightening concerns of war while I was at Fort Knox.

Unlike the Rock, Fort Knox was huge. I had driven to the base from home so I had transportation and could drive anywhere I needed to. The base was so large I had to use a map for the first month or so I was there. One of the first things I had to do was replace all my equipment and uniforms that I had left in Germany. I felt like such a bonehead having to tell my new platoon sergeant about this.

The barracks weren't quite as old as they were in Germany, but they were still old. The government was spending more money on the military but it was obvious none of it was going towards upgrading where we lived. There were a lot fewer people who had to live in the barracks because the married people had separate military housing available for them on post. There wasn't enough housing to accommodate all the families but there was a housing allowance available to help rent civilian housing in Ratcliff, Kentucky.

Fort Knox was in a dry county, but I could still buy alcohol on base. Since I was under the age of 21, I couldn't buy hard liquor but I could still buy beer. This didn't matter because I was done with all the drinking. I felt like I had done a lifetime's worth of it over there and, without realizing it, my priorities began changing the moment I arrived stateside. Suddenly, I found myself ready to settle down and start a family. Three months later I would be married, have a stepdaughter, and be renting a house in town. Ten months after that my twin sons would be born.

I was starting to see just how much those two demanding years in Germany had changed me. I had arrived over there a naïve, clueless kid, fresh out of basic training and I arrived here a mature, fully trained soldier. Events right after my arrival would further cement this newfound attitude. Unbeknownst to me, CPT Kranepuhl had awarded me the Army Achievement Medal (AAM) for my service in Germany. This was my first significant award and I was completely surprised when it was presented to me in front of my new company. Receiving this awoke something in me that made me want more awards. It lit a fire that would grow stronger with each future award. I became more focused and driven. I would soon be promoted to E-5 Sergeant, putting me into the leadership position of squad leader and firmly planting my feet on this new course. I now saw the military in a completely different light and began putting my entire focus on my career. I became consumed with the desire to succeed, placing my job above everything else.

I may not have been near the front line any more, but I still had to be prepared to go to war against the Soviets. In Germany, I had to be ready to mobilize immediately, without notice, to the Fulda Gap and prevent the Soviets from advancing until reinforcements arrived. The forces stationed in Europe couldn't withstand a soviet assault indefinitely and the United States would have to send additional forces from designated backup units stationed stateside. The 194th Armored Brigade at Fort Knox was one of these units. This meant I no longer had to live in a state of combat readiness every minute of every day, with a two-hour window to get back to post and locked and loaded in my vehicle. I was still an infantry soldier and would have to train just as hard, but it was so much easier when there wasn't a noose around my neck.

PT was still conducted as a company on Mondays, Wednesdays, and Fridays and as a platoon on Tuesdays and Thursdays. The necessity of remaining physically fit continued to be a priority. The objective now seemed to be to push me to complete muscle fatigue doing calisthenics and then running me until I felt like puking. For some reason, passing the semi-annual PT tests with 180 points just wasn't good enough for my new commanders, who expected scores of 270 or higher. This meant more push-ups and sit-ups and a quicker pace for the formation during those morning runs, always pushing me to my limits.

Fort Knox was so big that there were plenty of training options right there on base. There were firing ranges for most of the weapons found in an infantry unit so I no longer had to deploy just to fire them. There were large areas of both open and wooded terrain where I could train on tactics and land navigation without ever running into the base's fences. With the size of Fort Knox, overnight training exercises could be conducted year round without ever leaving the base and I spent many nights camped out in those woods.

I still had to endure countless road marches on foot. I was an infantry soldier and always had to be prepared for the contingency of not having a vehicle. The large expanses of Fort Knox and its many roads provided more opportunities than I liked for this.

I spent most my time training with the TOW system and the ITV, with a lot of time spent on target identification and tracking. A short distance from my motor pool, and just outside the Brandenburg gate on the northwest side of base, was a small area specifically set up for this training. It wasn't anything fancy, just a long hill that was high enough for the ITV's to line up behind and not be seen from the front to simulate being in a defensive position. Down range, a jeep would drive back and forth with the target board mounted on a pedestal. I spent a lot of time here target practicing and qualifying.

I got a break from my normal routines for one month every summer to be a trainer. Fort Knox would host military reservists and my unit was tasked with teaching them infantry skills. In a wooded area on the south side of post, a round robin of stations was set up for the reservists to rotate through. I was assigned to instruct them on the subject of observation posts (OP). I dug a full size, covered fox hole at my site, with every detail in place to illustrate exactly how it would look as specified in the manual. I gave a fifteen-minute lecture about OP's to each group as they rotated through each afternoon, explaining all the military standards for building and manning one. I conducted this lecture six to eight times each afternoon. Because the training was so successful, everyone involved received an Army Achievement Medal. This would be my second AAM.

During my second summer, I volunteered for the same subject. As luck would have it, my foxhole was still there and only needed small repairs to be ready and I didn't need to study much to be prepared for this block of instruction since I already knew the material. Because of this, I volunteered to be part of a demonstration on infantry tactics that was held each day before lunch. The reservists were seated in bleachers and shown the different formations the infantry uses when moving on foot while someone explained each formation. The demonstration ended with a simulated combat assault using blanks and smoke grenades to add realism. I would return to my OP station to conduct the round robin block of instruction each afternoon.

Once again, everyone involved in this teaching would receive an AAM for their efforts. Everyone except me that is. My battalion commander decided since I had received the award the previous year I shouldn't get a second one. He gave me a Department of Defense Certificate of Achievement instead. This is when I first realized how out of touch battalion commanders were with the front-line soldiers in their command. Unfortunately, I would see this throughout my career.

My unit deployed to Fort Drum in New York for a month of training in the fall of 1983. I was attending the Primary Non-commissioned Officers Course on base when they deployed. They were still gone when I graduated so I was assigned to the battalion rear detachment. Part of my responsibilities were to take care of the company supply room until they got back. Most of my time was spent picking up trash around base, painting, and deep cleaning the common areas in my barracks. I spent a lot of time working the floor buffers to strip and wax those hallways and offices to keep busy. It was during this time that I would experience the tragedy of death firsthand when someone I knew very well from my platoon was killed.

One morning word was received that there had been an accident at Fort Drum and a soldier had been killed. The identity of the soldier was at first withheld until his family could be notified. I was soon informed that it was PFC Dozier, the driver of my squad's ITV and one of my roommates until I had moved off base. He was a great guy and well-liked by everyone. The accident happened during a training exercise at night. The unit was practicing a combat road march that required all vehicle lights to be turned off for stealth. Armored vehicles had a small red light mounted on the back of each vehicle so that drivers have something to see when following another vehicle without being seen by the enemy. It was while they had been conducting one of these movements that he was killed. The convoy was crossing a bridge and when he attempted it, one side of the ITV track missed the bridge causing the vehicle to roll down a ravine. He had been killed instantly. His gear was expedited back to base and his personal items bagged and sent to the supply room. One of the more difficult things I ever did while in the army was processing his belongings to be forwarded to his family.

Chapter 14
Leadership

When I arrived at Fort Knox I was getting close to being eligible for promotion to E-5, the rank of Sergeant. I had to attend the Primary Leadership Development Course (PLDC) before I could be promoted to this leadership position. This course was conducted in a basic training-type atmosphere, designed to challenge me mentally and physically. I was required to move in to the school's barracks for the duration of the course.

The focus of the school was to teach enlisted soldiers the necessary knowledge and basic skills to be leaders. I was taught and tested on the many different army regulations covering leadership. They retrained me on important infantry skills to expand my knowledge in these areas while teaching this from a leadership perspective. And of course, I had to pass the standard physical fitness test.

PT was conducted most mornings and I wore fatigue pants, t-shirt and combat boots. As I had expected, I was pushed to my limits during the calisthenics portion before going on a short run of two to three miles. This would have been an easy run if I hadn't been wearing combat boots. All these demands placed upon me physically were always necessary because my job required it for survival. As a leader in the infantry, physical fitness would become even more important because I needed to be able to lead by example. Falling out of formation from fatigue or whining about my pain while road marching was not the example the army wanted its leaders to set.

One of the course requirements was to be able to conduct the calisthenics portion of PT. This was important because the responsibility for leading PT in my company was rotated by platoon and I would need to be able to conduct it properly when called upon. To learn this, each morning I had to take turns with my classmates in front of the formation, leading the different exercises until the instructor passed me on it. I enjoyed my time leading these sessions so I learned how to do it quickly. It's funny how easy I could learn new things when I enjoyed it.

I was even more surprised to learn how much I liked singing the cadence during the morning runs. I wasn't blessed with a good singing voice, not even in the shower, so I never, ever sang in front of anybody unless I had lots of alcohol in me. I sang quite a bit in Germany.

When running in formation, songs are sung to a distinct rhythm to keep everyone in step. As expected with a bunch of young men, most of the songs centered on women, drinking, and just plain raunchiness with very colorful lyrics. There weren't very many women in the army and none in the combat units so a few of the lyrics were pretty derogatory towards them. This was starting to change though and it and would eventually be banned from being sung on base by commanders. These songs were just silly little humorous versus that soldiers could relate to.

Singing cadence is nothing like singing a song. To me it seemed more like a combination of singing loudly and shouting. The words flowed from my mouth like a song but it felt like I was hollering them. I may not be able to sing but I found out I was good at hollering. I have a naturally loud voice and big lungs so it was like I was born to sing cadence. I enjoyed leading formations and singing the running songs. This was something I would do at every opportunity throughout my career from this point on. It never occurred to me that I wasn't any good at it so I might owe an apology to lots of guys I served with.

Running at PLDC wasn't limited just to PT. The mess hall was located a short distance from the classrooms and I had to run in formation to it every day for all three meals. This would have been an easy task if it weren't so hot at lunch and dinner times. I dreaded those short runs to the mess hall even more than the morning PT runs.

I also spent time learning the rules and regulations covering drill and ceremonies. Not only did I need to know these regulations inside and out, I needed to know how to lead a formation. To practice, we took turns marching each other around a parking lot, barking the various orders to guide the formation, while calling out the cadence to keep everyone in step. Calling out the cadence was done in a loud voice, almost a shout. Not so surprisingly, it came naturally to me. Like singing cadence during PT, this turned out to be something else I enjoyed. After this school, I would volunteer to leading the formations and call the marching cadence every chance I could.

There are numerous types of formations used regularly by units and I had to know how to execute all of them. For exercising, the soldiers had to be moved from the standard marching formation, to open ranks to space everyone out evenly and gave plenty of room for each person to exercise. I didn't want to kick the guy next to me in the head when I exercised nor did I particularly want to feel his boot upside mine. There were inspection formations that allowed commanders to move easily down each row checking uniforms and weapons. There were formations for marching, running, and parades. I had to be able to give the proper commands to move the group in and out of these formations. Most of us learned it quickly, but a few had to build their confidence up to leading a group. We practiced this in our favorite parking lot whenever there was spare time until everyone was good at it.

As a Non-commissioned Officer (NCO) and a leader, I would be responsible for the training and preparation of the soldiers assigned to me. I had to be able to speak in front of a group without fear if I wanted to be successful at this. To prepare for this responsibility, there was time allocated for me to practice and then be tested on properly giving an oral presentation to the class. This turned out to be something else I have a natural talent for, making it easy for me. I found out I was good at giving a presentation or teaching a subject from memory once I had learned the materials, a talent that would serve me well throughout my military career and beyond.

Fort Knox was a convenient location for PLDC with its acres upon acres of wooded areas within its boundaries. These woods provided an exceptional area for the advanced land navigation training conducted at PLDC. I could walk for miles and never see any signs of civilization. To the untrained eye - everything looked the same - with tree after tree as far as the eye could see. But with the proper training and a map, a protractor, and a compass, the course taught me how to read the terrain and to navigate my way around as if I were traveling through a city.

I have always had a knack for finding my way around no matter where I was. This made the land navigation easy for me to understand and I mastered it quickly. My commander in Germany had taught me a lot about map reading and how to navigate from a vehicle, giving me an advantage over my class when this was being taught. I would need to be very proficient in these advanced land navigation skills to be in a leadership position. I was instructed on how to read terrain so that I could travel in difficult environments where everything seemed to look the same. To graduate, I had to successfully complete a very difficult land navigation course on my own as part of the requirements to graduate. This was a very important skill to have in the infantry in a time before cell phones and GPS's.

The course was in a very dense, hilly wooded area. I was given multiple coordinates to find in a specific order and a time limit for finishing the course. The first thing I had to do was mark all the coordinates I was given on the map. I then drew lines to each coordinate with my protractor in the order I had to follow, I calculated the distance and the azimuth (degree on my compass to follow) from each one. At each coordinate, I would find a white stake in the ground with a number painted on it that had to be recorded on the test sheet to verify I had found it. Using my azimuth for direction, I would match the terrain on the ground to the map and head to the next coordinate. It seemed like looking for a needle in a haystack, but with the lessons I had just learned, I eventually reached the last coordinate and finish line with time to spare. This was an awesome feeling, reaching the end after being out all day by myself, searching for those stakes.

I successfully completed PLDC and was promoted to sergeant a few months later. The course taught the basic principles and standards of leadership and prepare soldiers for the transition into leadership positions. The practical application of leading was the responsibility of the unit NCO's. I was blessed to have some great ones in my immediate chain-of-command at Fort Knox to learn from. My first sergeant was 1SG Anderson and my platoon sergeant was SFC Troy Dickerson, both of whom were great examples for a newly promoted NCO like myself. I couldn't have asked for better people to show me how to be a good leader. 1SG Anderson would also be my first sergeant for a short period at my next duty station.

SFC Dickerson, like CPT Kranepuhl, took me under his wing and became my mentor. He taught me that being a leader wasn't about power and barking orders but leading by example. He made his soldiers want to be their best without raising his voice, teaching me that I could get more out of my soldiers from respect than fear. He like to use whimsical sayings to make his point and one he used often was, "It's easier to catch flies with honey than vinegar." Another expression he liked was, "I'm so hungry I could sap the sore off a hog's butt with a dry biscuit." I never understood that one. He used the example of leading with an iron fist in a velvet glove, emphasizing the velvet glove. A good leader needed to be willing to use the iron fist so his soldiers knew it was there even though they only saw the velvet glove. I would still have to bring the hammer down occasionally, but not as often if I had the respect of my soldiers. My time with him made me become the successful leader I would become. All the accomplishment in my military career can be traced back to my time with him and I will forever be grateful.

Chapter 15
National Training Center

Fort Irwin, California became the National Training Center for the army in 1980. Located in the Mojave Desert, the base provided miles and miles of desert for armored vehicles to maneuver freely in a secure environment away from prying eyes. An Opposing Force (OPFOR) was established utilizing a detachment of soldiers from the 6th Battalion, 31st Infantry and 1st Battalion, 73rd Armor Divisions of the 7th Infantry Division at Fort Ord. These battalions were attached to a newly formed unit, the 32nd Guards Motorized Rifle Regiment known as the 32nd MRR (G) at Fort Irwin.

The OPFOR was tasked with the responsibility of representing Soviet forces in war games against units that rotated through the training center. The base maintained a collection of soviet tanks and armored personnel carriers. Some of the tanks they used were the older Patton tanks disguised to look like Soviet tanks. Everything they did was to duplicate the Soviets on the battlefield, down to the smallest detail, including the uniforms they wore and the tactics they used. They trained year round for this and were nearly impossible to beat.

By the time I went to Fort Irwin, technology continued to improve. The military had just introduced the Multiple Integrated Laser Engagement System, known as MILES, and my unit was one of the first to use it at Fort Irwin. Targets could be tracked and acquired in real time, making combat training exercises much more realistic. It eliminated any delay in removing vehicles and personnel from training exercises once they were hit by a laser.

Prior to beginning the exercise, a large yellow flashing light was mounted on the rear of each vehicle and connected to a small data box inside the vehicle. Large straps were attached horizontally around each vehicle using Velcro and connected to a data box that was mounted inside. The straps had large, button-like sensors on them that would set off the alarm and flashing light when hit by a laser. A vehicle whose light was flashing had to stop where it was until it was reset for the next battle.

For weapon systems that had a targeting sight, like those used on the ITV's and tanks, there was a specially designed sight that shot a laser at any target when triggered. Another small box was attached to the end of the M16 rifle that emitted a smaller laser for engaging opposing ground troops. Soldiers wore a special harness that had small sensors and a buzzer that would go off when hit by a small weapon laser. A rifle laser couldn't take out an armored vehicle because the laser wasn't strong enough to trigger the sensors on the vehicle. This was all very similar to what kids now use for laser tag.

But I need to be clear here. The MILES system was an awesome upgrade to combat training in 1984 but it didn't have any impact on my drive to beat the OPFOR. It didn't matter whether it was lasers, painted signs, or big sticks and pine cone hand grenades, I wanted to win. We all did. We hated the Soviets with a passion and since the OPFOR represented them, they had to be beaten.

I deployed to Fort Irwin my first year at Fort Knox after spending months preparing for it. I flew out of Louisville on a Military C-130's and it was my first time to fly in a military plane. Each plane had pallets of equipment secured down the center and web seating that ran along both sides of the plane. The rear of the plane was left clear. There were paratroopers from Fort Bragg onboard who would be training with us and they would be parachuting out the back of the plane just before it landed at Fort Irwin. As the plane neared the drop zone, I got to watch as they all lined up in single file and left the plane.

My entire time at Fort Irwin was very demanding. I had only been a sergeant and a section leader for about two and a half months, and this felt like my first big test. As soon as all the equipment was loaded onto the vehicles, we started training on offensive and defensive techniques to get familiar with maneuvering and hiding in this desert environment. The ITV had hatches over the driver and the gunner seats that were opened for most of the time when we were moving. The driver's seat was raised high enough so that his head stuck out when he was driving. The squad or section leader stood on the gunner's seat, giving him a clear view to navigate. Everyone wore head gear that plugged into a communication system so that each could talk and hear each other. This system was also connected to the radio.

After about a week of training in the desert, the battles began. The exercise was designed to replicate war conditions so a combat readiness state had to be maintained for the rest of the deployment, constantly vigilant for enemy activity. Security shifts were conducted every night, even when we were set up in an assembly area preparing for battles. Full combat gear was worn over my MOPP pants and jacket at all times and every task had to be conducted as if it were in a hostile environment.

I went through many different battle scenarios like what I did at Reforger in Germany, rotating between exercises as part of the defending forces and then the aggressors on offense. I would be briefed on the mission specifics as they related to my platoon before each battle and then I oversaw the preparation of my guys for the implementation of it in the upcoming battle.

On offense, my platoon would maneuver through the desert until contact was made with the OPFOR. I would move my squad into positions to engage them and the battle would start in earnest. The desert quickly began filling up with blinking yellow lights as vehicles were taken out. Push and pull, give and take, these mock battles would rage on just like a real war. The battle would eventually end and both sides would regroup to prepare for this next battle. I usually had an idea who won from the amount of blinking lights I could see around me and it usually wasn't my side.

Being on defense required much more work. I had to find a small hill or berm in my assigned area that would give the vehicle the most natural protection and concealment. The vehicle had a large camouflage net that was then erected over it to help blend in with the terrain. A forward observation post (OP) had to be built using sandbags if time permitted. I was never given the time of each attack so I would assign guard duties and rotate the guys on shifts in the OP.

The MILES made these mock battles more realistic and the OPFOR made it more challenging. We were outnumbered and outsmarted by a foe that was trained in both American and Soviet tactics and knew the terrain far better than we ever could. I trained to win so losing these battles ticked me off, pushing me harder in the next battle. Dying was worse than losing and my heart would sink into my stomach when the light on the vehicle started blinking or the buzzer on my web gear went off. The most humiliating thing in the world was stopping where I was and having to watch my fellow soldiers fight on.

It happened to everyone at some point and I remember one time that it happened to me when I was on defense. I had just completed preparing and we had done an excellent job camouflaging the ITV. While waiting in anticipation for the excitement to begin, I was looking through the periscope, searching for signs of the OPFOR vehicles to my front. Out of nowhere, the buzzers on everybody's gear unexpectedly started going off. An OPFOR infantry unit had sneaked up on foot from behind me and taken my entire squad out. I didn't live this down for a long time.

The Fort Irwin National Training Center was designed to give units a real-world experience of fighting a war with the Soviets. This provided units with a well-trained enemy that knew the battlefield. A foe that had been in countless similar battles with previous units, gaining them an edge that made them impossible to defeat. I think we lost every battle. I knew that winning wasn't necessarily the intent of the training exercises but I still wanted to win.

The officers at the top of my chain of command designed each battle plan before passing it down until it reached the platoon levels. The platoon leaders were at the bottom of the pecking order, as far as officers went, and they were responsible for the actual execution these plans by the soldiers. Nobody likes to lose, which was motivation enough for me. To the officers, losing meant their plans didn't work so they created unnecessary pressure on all of us while we prepared. This made the constant losing more depressing and very overwhelming at times. I went through a period of loathing and feeling like I had let everyone down if I did get killed in the exercise. It was far better seeing that yellow light flashing and being able to learn from my mistakes. This would allow me to better prepare for the real thing where there would be no second chances.

I think this was the whole point, to provide an experience as close as possible to an actual battle with the Soviets. Each time my light started flashing or my buzzers went off, I learned invaluable lessons that made me better at my job. I wanted to win and took dying seriously, even make believe dying, so with each subsequent confrontation with the OPFOR, I did get better, we all did. After the war games, I had a much clearer idea of what I would be up against in a confrontation with the Soviets, something I realized I never had when I was stationed close to them in Germany.

The military was starting to evolve now. With the defense budget no longer being burned up in a war, money could be funneled towards new technology. The ITV was now fully integrated into the army. The M1 Abrams tank and the M2 Bradley Fighting Vehicle were being introduced as the new generation of armored vehicles. All of the older M60A1 Patton tanks had been replaced by the Abrams and the Bradley was replacing all of the armored personnel carriers that had been around for years.

These upgrades that were sweeping through the army were designed to replace the older, outdated vehicles with more technologically advanced ones. Mechanized units were slow by nature and it took time to move from position to position. The Abrams and the Bradley were faster, allowing units to be more mobile. Fort Irwin provided an excellent place to test the newer vehicles and to give units' experience practicing tactics with them against a realistic enemy. Watching the

Abrams tanks flying across the desert, chasing down opposing vehicles, was an amazing thing to see. The speeds they were traveling at were phenomenal compared to the M60 Patton tanks. Seeing them in action made it obvious these tanks were superior to anything the Soviets had and I couldn't help but feel proud.

Vehicles and equipment weren't the only improvements being seen. The army seemed to have finally used up its inventory of C-rations and replaced it with MRE's (Meals Ready to Eat). There was a variety of different meals available and they all looked and tasted like real food. I enjoyed eating them and it was much easier to trade for my favorites. The entrée came in a plastic bag that could be placed in boiling water if I wanted to warm it up but I usually didn't take the time to do this because, even cold, MRE's were so much better than C-Rations. Tobasco Sauce and Cheese Wiz were still staples to liven up the monotony of eating them all the time but they weren't needed as often. In fact, it was common for guys to snack on MRE's back at Fort Knox, something I never saw with C-Rations.

Hot meals were still a luxury that I looked forward to each day. I was served a hot breakfast and dinner most days but lunch was always an MRE. The unit cooks prepared meals in a rear assembly area that were delivered to our positions. The meals were served in tactical chow lines to simulated eating in a hostile environment. The serving containers were placed in covered positions at least ten meters apart because a hand grenade has a ten-meter kill zone. A line was formed leading to the food with the same distance between each soldier. A covered position that provided camouflage was used if it were close to this distance and available. As I waited to move forward, I would have to lie in a prone position, rifle aimed outward, until the person in front of me moved. Once he got into position at the next spot, I would sprint to the position he just left, repeating this until I had been through each serving station. I then had to find a spot the same ten-meter distance from anyone else, and eat alone.

When thinking of the desert, I expected it to be hot and dry. This was kind of true in January and the days were usually very warm. My MOPP gear was worn the entire time since this was combat training, making it even warmer. The desert made it safe for the limited use of real tear gas to make the training for chemical and biological attacks more realistic. The Soviets were likely to use chemical weapons in a war, so the OPFOR utilized the gas as part of their tactics. I encountered it a few times, experiencing the burning eyes and lungs, leading me frantically put on my gas mask.

The temperatures dropped significantly at night to below freezing. The only source of warmth I had was in my sleeping bag which was designed to be used in Arctic temperatures and more than adequate for the cold Mojave nights. Sleeping in clothes causes them to get damp with sweat and would make me even colder when they were exposed to the cold air in the morning. I was supposed to strip down to my skivvies and sleep with them inside my bag to prevent this from happening. I didn't spend much time sleeping during these exercises and didn't want to waste time getting in and out of my uniform, so I slept in it anyway. I would climb into my bag and fold it over me with my boots sticking out the end and cherish those extra minutes of sleep this saved me. I had to sleep in the vehicle in full gear during combat exercises at night. The driver would sleep in his seat, and the loader and squad leader slept sitting on the bench in the rear cargo area, and the gunner slept in the turret. I had to take turns rotating guard shifts with the other three guys and sit in the squad leader's seat looking through the periscope for signs of enemy activity. I was usually so tired that I passed out as soon as it was allowed until my turn to be on watch.

Most military attacks throughout history happened during the time just before sunrise. This was because soldiers are more likely to be disorganized when first awakened and during the early moments that followed. The temperature typically drops to its coldest level just before the sun breaks the horizon, providing another distraction.

To prevent this from happening, my day always started at least an hour before sunrise when the last person on guard duty would wake me up. The first thing I had to do was shave. That's right, I shaved. The army maintained that a gas mask wouldn't seal properly to a face with stubble so I had to shave every morning of everyday no matter where I was. I would pour cold water into my helmet and lather up in total darkness. Mirrors weren't allowed because they reflect light and could give up my location, so I would sit down on the ground and use my hands to feel and guide my razor.

The one thing I missed the most on this deployment had to be showers. Halfway through the training and again at the end of it, I was taken to a field shower site where a tent had been set up with rows of showers inside. And hot water! I had to wait in a long line to use it, but it was worth the wait. Once it was my turn, I was given five minutes to remove weeks of grime, which didn't leave much time to enjoy the feel of that glorious hot water beating down on my tired body.

I wasn't an animal and did clean myself as best I could between these showers by taking what was referred to as a "whore's bath" whenever the time allowed for it. I'd fill my helmet with cold water, remove my shirt, and use a wash cloth and soap to clean as much dirt and sweat off as I could. If I felt extremely dirty and had the time, I would remove everything and wash my entire body this way. In extended downtime, it wasn't uncommon to see someone off in the distance, standing there in all his glory, washing away.

The other thing I missed was something I took for granted until I didn't have it: a toilet. Most of my deployments took me to wooded areas which offered trees for concealment while taking care of this business. Holes could be dug under fallen trees to make a primitive throne for some comfort. Not in the desert where there was no such thing as privacy. I could only hope for a small hill to hide behind and prayed nobody drove by while nature called. Inevitably somebody would and all I could do was smile and nod like squatting over a hole was the most natural thing in the world. I always took these side excursions on my own and hoped for some privacy. There were always a few guys who must have had little bit of a female gene in them because they had no problem going on these trips at the same time, digging their hole a few feet away and in my line of sight. This wouldn't have been so awkward if they didn't try holding a conversation the whole time as well.

Chapter 16
Big Changes

My sons were born on May 20, 1984 at Ireland Army Community Hospital, Fort Knox, Kentucky. They were fraternal twins and supposed to be a boy and girl. I had wanted a son to name after me and got two instead. So, my firstborn came into this world at seven pounds and was named Robert Allen Kern Jr. Thirty minutes later my second firstborn son made an entrance at four pounds ten ounces. I named him Robby Allen Kern. Bobby and Robby. Bob and Rob.

Robby, being so small, was considered a premature baby and had to stay in the hospital a few more days until he gained some weight. The doctors noticed something wrong with his heart and after months of testing, he was diagnosed with Coarctation of the Aorta, a narrowing of the main artery leading out of the heart. One of his symptoms was extremely low blood pressure in his legs.

I was approaching the end of my four-year enlistment when this diagnoses was finally made. I discussed my future with Mom and realized reenlisting made sense with three very young children, especially considering that Robby's medical issues were going to require continual monitoring by doctors. It was an easy decision and I enjoyed the Army now that I was in a leadership position. After spending a short time considering my options, I committed myself to continuing the cause and, during the fall of 1984, I reenlisted for another four years. Unlike when I first enlisted, there were no bonuses being offered as incentives for infantry soldiers to reenlist. I did get the reenlistment officer to find an infantry slot open in Hawaii and had this assignment guaranteed in my contract. Might as well live in paradise for a while.

The tension between the east and west was at its worst then and war with the Soviets still seemed inevitable. Communism continued rearing its ugly head in smaller countries with the Soviets pulling the strings and influencing governments. President Reagan was willing to openly support the opposition to thwart these efforts, and as we now know, not so openly. Weapons and support were given to contra rebels in Nicaragua as they fought to overthrow a communist government. A small force of United States soldiers was sent to the tiny island of Grenada to overthrow that communist government and keep the Soviets from building an airstrip on the island. President Reagan's refusal to negotiate with terrorism is believed to have led to the growth of international terrorism such as the horrific attack in Lebanon when a suicide bomber drove a truck full of explosives into a marine barracks. World events seemed to be skirting the abyss during this time, with numerous hotspots that any one of them could provide the spark to begin World War III.

I was scheduled to transfer to Hawaii in April of 1985. Towards the end of 1984, Robby's doctors decided it was time to schedule surgery to correct his heart problem so that he would be recovered enough for the flight to Hawaii. His brother was already standing and attempting to walk yet he was showing no signs of even trying to do this. The surgery was scheduled at Walter Reed Army Medical Center in Washington DC in February 1985. I was given three weeks of convalescent leave so that I could drive him there for the surgery.

January 1985 was spent training in a desert in Idaho. This was a very similar environment to Fort Irwin except there wasn't a simulated soviet OPFOR to train against. It was further north than Fort Irwin and the Mojave Desert so it was much colder. These exercises were more in line with what I did at Hohenfels in Germany only in a desert environment.

I don't remember anything significant about my thirty days in this desert except how cold it was. I can think of several reasons for this and at the top of this list would have to be my concern about the heart surgery Robby was scheduled to have when I got back. The boys were barely seven months old when I left for Idaho. They were both happy little guys that brought so much joy to me. It was terrifying thinking about him going through the surgery. This weighed heavily on me from the moment I found out about his heart problem. Knowing when the doctors were going to finally try to fix him made me worry constantly. There wasn't anybody that I could share this with, so I shouldered it quietly while I threw myself into my job.

The training itself was as intense as I had expected, maybe a little harder because of the cold temperatures, but it had less of an impact on me than previous deployments. I had been an E-5 sergeant and a section leader for over a year by this time and saw everything from a different perspective. The promotion to sergeant caused a transformation in me that changed my entire focus to making my job my top priority. I became somewhat of a perfectionist in everything I did because I wanted to be a better leader and set a good example. I tried to work harder than everyone else, which meant longer work days for me and coming in on days off to check on my guys and spend time with them. I also wanted to make SFC Dickerson proud of me.

I was completely comfortable in my role as section leader by this time. I was now the one responsible for teaching and pushing my guys to their limits and I relished this responsibility. I was less aware of everything around me because I was more focused on our assignments and responsibilities. As a section leader, I participated in the planning and development of each training exercise for the platoon, and then the implementation and execution of it. This kept my attention focused on each task and I was less aware of anything outside of this bubble.

Another reason this deployment was less memorable was because I was in great shape. I had been in the army for almost four years and I was more accustomed to the physical demands. It was still hard, but it was now more routine, more second nature, so I could go through the motions without much thought. I could no longer complain about my circumstances because I was involved in creating them. Besides, the army frowned upon leaders who whined. So, when my feet, legs, or my whole body hurt, I suffered in silence because that's what good leaders did.

We spent a lot of time practicing the different offensive maneuvers as a platoon in this desert environment. I had to set up defensive positions and spent hours running through our targeting procedures. There were countless company convoys in combat formations to different regions of the desert. I had to wear my MOPP suit for most of the training and I still got cold, especially when I was standing up in the gunner's seat during convoys and maneuvers. It's the only time I can remember wearing it and not overheating. Did I mention it was cold?

One thing I do remember well was all the badger holes. They were everywhere. We were briefed on badgers before departing Fort Knox because they are quite abundant in Idaho, particularly in the desert area. They lived in holes and their claws were as sharp as razors. I was warned to be cautious around these holes so that I didn't step in one and tear up a leg or ankle, and to always be aware of the occupants of the hole. I never did see a badger despite all the holes I saw.

I was warned not to be lazy and use one of these holes for a latrine instead of digging my own hole. Badgers don't like being awakened by GI's dropping stinky bombs down into their homes. There were rumors flying around about a guy in another company doing this and getting sliced badly on his bum. Personally, I think this rumor was started just to keep anyone from trying this. It was enough of a warning for me: I wouldn't even dig a hole anywhere in sight of another hole. A tough task considering there were holes everywhere you looked. Based upon the number of holes I saw, there must have been a million badgers living in that desert.

When it finally came time to head back home, there was this huge, single file line I had to wait in to load my vehicle onto the train for the trip home. It felt like this was the coldest night of our deployment and I spent hours in this line. I don't ever remember being as miserable as I was that night. I would sometimes stand on top of my vehicle and put our legs over the exhaust pipe for heat. The exhaust fumes would blow up my pant legs and jacket, inflating them slightly while the hot air toasted my entire body. I am very lucky I didn't poison myself breathing in all those exhaust fumes that were heating me up.

A few weeks after returning, I took my son to Washington, DC. I decided to drive because it was cheaper than flying. Somewhere in Pennsylvania I was questioning this decision when my transmission went out. It was a cold, rainy night as I rolled to a stop in the middle of nowhere, confident my trip was over and the surgery would have to be rescheduled. It turned out that I must have broken down in Mayberry. A police officer stopped and then contacted someone in town who worked on transmission. He arranged for a wrecker to get the car to him and then loaded my wife, my son and myself into his car and took us to a motel across the street from where my car was being fixed. A transmission was found the next morning, and after one more night in the motel, I was back on the road to DC.

I arrived in DC that evening, only a day late, but in time for the surgery. I checked-in to the Ronald McDonald House and the next morning I went to Walter Reed Army Medical Center and checked Robby in. On the day of surgery, sitting in the waiting room while my baby boy was undergoing surgery on his heart was the most difficult thing I ever had to endure. The doctor finally came out and told me that the surgery was a success. Soon after, I got to go see him in the recovery room where I saw one of the happiest sights I have ever seen. There was my son with all these tubes and wires stuck all over his body, standing straight up in his crib. Just a few hours after open heart surgery and there he was standing for the first time in his life. The most memorable thing was the huge grin on his face when he saw me enter the room. I still get emotional all these years later just thinking about it.

His recovery went well and I was given the doctor's approval to depart as scheduled for Hawaii if Robby was seen by a heart spe-

106

cialist when I got there. In a miraculous twist of fate, Robby's surgeon had been reassigned to Tripler Army Medical Center in Hawaii and would be his doctor for the upcoming years.

The time finally arrived and I departed Fort Knox with my family. We drove to Charlotte, North Carolina where I dropped my car off to be put on a boat for Hawaii. I enjoyed Fort Knox because of how close it was to home, but I was excited to be heading to Hawaii for the next three years. Hawaii was paradise, at least to me. This assignment was the toughest of my career turned out to be the most physical and difficult assignment of them all. But I loved my time in Hawaii, despite the hard training,

Chapter 17
Schofield Barracks

In April of 1985, the spread of communism was still our biggest concern, the Soviets remained our biggest enemy, and President Reagan was having none of it. We were beginning to see a slight shift in the Cold War with the Soviets. In 1984, the United States Strategic Defense Initiative was introduced to shift our focus from having the most nuclear weapons as a deterrent to a nuclear war. This program was initiated to develop a defense system for the United States to protect us from a nuclear attack including the development of missiles that could be launched from space. President Reagan was at the height of his popularity in his second term. In 1985, when I arrived at Schofield Barracks Mikhail Gorbachev had taken over in the Soviet Union and we would begin seeing cracks in their armor. These two would meet and set the course for bring the Soviets into the light. After decades of funneling money into their oversized military, the country and the Soviet government were beginning to crumble.

Rocky IV would be released in late 1985 using the Cold War as the theme. Ivan Drago was the villain and embodied everything we hated about communism. We mourned as a nation when Drago killed the beloved Apollo Creed in the ring and we seethed at his emotionless response. Entire theaters erupted with cheers when Rocky beat Drago in the end, and the sight of Rocky draped in the American flag brought tears to our eyes. Most people who lived through the Cold War era still have these strong reactions when watching this movie today. For those of us who served in the military during this period, these emotions are even stronger. Stallone had used more than just Rocky's underdog persona to move us. He found a way to play on our national pride using our hatred for communism as the emotional draw.

I mention this movie because the reaction this movie brings out in most people is a great example of why most of us served. We wanted to help take the Dragos of the world down.

But the Cold War remained at its highest levels of concern at this time. War seemed imminent and a nuclear war still a very strong possibility. We were starting to see The People's Republic of China emerge as a military power. They had their own arsenal of nuclear weapons and the largest military in the world - reputed to be a million-man army. There were also a couple of communist countries in the Asian Pacific that were supported by the Soviets and China that were a concern to us. These countries were allies of the Soviets and had given communism a foothold in the region. In Hawaii, our primary mission was to be prepared to deploy to any of these hotspots if needed to prevent communism from spreading any further in this part of the world.

One of the communist threats in this region was Vietnam. In the early years of communism, Vietnam had been divided with the communist portion of the country located in the north. At the end of the Vietnam War in 1975, South Vietnam fell and Vietnam become one communist country. Because communism has a history of growing through conquering neighboring countries, the countries in the region feared the same fate. The United States and Thailand held annual joint military exercises known as Cobra Gold to show our support to the area and enable us to become familiar with the area by conducting actual training there.

Lastly there was North Korea, a communist country that remains a thorn in our side to this day. North Korean became a nuclear country with the help of the Soviets. In the early 1980's, Korea began trying to develop nuclear weapons, making them an even bigger threat to the region. Since the end of the Korean War, the U.S. has maintained a force in South Korea to help defend the border from another attack from the north. A joint exercise in South Korea known as Team Spirit was conducted to practice different scenarios of an invasion from the north. This was an annual training exercise that the 25th Infantry Division participated in every year. Different units of the division would fly there and conduct combat training exercises with the South Korean Army. Like Reforger in Germany, Team Spirit was just as much a training exercise as it was a show of force to the North Koreans. It was also a show of support to the South Koreans who shared a border with a communist neighbor that always seemed to have a lunatic as their leader. A lunatic trying to develop a nuclear weapon.

I never considered any of this when I reenlisted. I just wanted to live in paradise and felt fortunate to be doing it on Uncle Sam's dime. I seemed to have forgotten that life in the infantry was never going to be sunshine and rainbows.

Arriving in Honolulu was exactly as I had dreamed it would be. Leaving the airport, I could see palm trees and flowers everywhere I turned. This really was paradise. I have been to southern Florida dozens of times in my life and yet it didn't come close to what it felt like in Hawaii. There is a uniqueness to that island air, the feel and smell of it that is hard to explain. My daughter had recently turned three and the boys were only eleven months old when I got there and were far too young to appreciate any of this. They were just happy to finally be off the airplane.

We were placed in temporary housing until a three-bedroom unit became available on base. The housing was nothing fancy and looked like an old hotel that had been converted into apartment-type units for incoming military families. It was in Pearl City which is the city adjacent to Pearl Harbor. My apartment faced the Harbor and it had an awesome view. Looking out you couldn't help but feel all the history there. If you climbed on the walkway rails and leaned far enough out, you could see the USS Arizona Memorial. Simply awesome!

My personal vehicle wasn't due in for a few weeks so I rented a car to make the daily commute to Schofield Barracks. I loved these morning drives to work. These first few weeks I had no idea of how intense my time stationed here would be so those morning drives were carefree. I loved driving down the short highway with the beautiful mounds of Bougainvillea flowers of lavender and pink and palm trees lining both sides of the highway as far as the eye could see. To my left I could catch glimpses of the beautiful ocean most of the way. Traffic was always light, allowing me to take in this panoramic view and enjoy its beauty every morning.

The trips back to Pearl City weren't quite as pleasant but I still enjoyed them. Traffic was always heavy, requiring my full attention. I would drive with the window down so I could enjoy that warm island air with it sweet aroma flowing through the car. This was Hawaii so why should I stress over heavy traffic.

I was assigned to the Headquarters Company, 1st Battalion, 5th Infantry Regiment of the 1st Brigade in the 25th Infantry Division at Schofield Barracks. In January of 1986 my unit was renamed to 3rd Battalion, 21st Infantry Regiment. The 25th Infantry Division had a primary mission to be ready to deploy anywhere in the Pacific Basin if ordered. The division was nicknamed Tropic Lightning for its successes in World War II. Like my last unit, my new company consisted of an anti-tank platoon, a scout platoon, a mortar platoon, and a headquarters platoon. I was pleasantly surprised to find 1SG Anderson who had been my First Sergeant at Fort Knox was the First Sergeant for my new company.

To the rear of Schofield Barracks is the famous Kolekole Pass that the Japanese planes flew around on their way to Pearl Harbor. Schofield Barracks and neighboring Wheeler Air Base were the first to be hit by the waves of Japanese planes on their way to Pearl Harbor. Some of the barracks still had the holes in the concrete walls where bullets from the Japanese planes had hit. I always thought they must have been left unpatched as a memorial or reminder of this world-changing event in American history. This part of history was main reason I had requested Hawaii when I reenlisted. I had done my senior term paper on the attack on Pearl Harbor so all this history was especially interesting to me.

My unit had just gotten back from Team Spirit when I arrived. I conducted the in-processing to my unit while they were recovering their equipment from this deployment. By the time I finished visiting all the appropriate stations and signing for my gear, they were finished as well. My platoon sergeant introduced me to the squad I would be in charge of and showed me around. This was not an armored division as I had been accustomed to so there were no ITV's, Bradley Fighting Vehicles or Abram Tanks. I was now assigned to an actual grunt unit where the infantry soldiers traveled on foot and my platoon used Jeeps to transport our TOW weapon systems. There was a pedestal mounted in back that replaced the tripod of the TOW. The rest of the system still consisted of the regular ground components which were the traverse, launch tube, and the day and night sights. There was a rack to the side that housed the missiles. Once again I found myself having to learn a new procedure for my job and the undesirable reality of being a newbie in the platoon. It didn't matter that I was a sergeant and in charge of my own squad, I was still a newbie when I got there. Fortunately, it was an easy transition from the ITV to a Jeep since the Jeep was a pretty basic set up with the TOW system. The squad responsibilities were much simpler without all the technology on an ITV.

The physical demands placed upon me here would be the biggest difference with this assignment. My job was still to support the infantry companies in the battalion whose primary mode of transportation was by foot. I found out right away that physical fitness was going to be taken to a whole new level here.

Chapter 18
Grunt Fitness

Each unit in the army has its own unit guidon, or flag, that is carried with the unit commander everywhere he goes. The guidon is always to the front of the unit and to the right of the commander in marching and running formations. The commanding general was Major General Kicklighter when I arrived at Schofield Barracks. The general was very high on individual soldier fitness and readiness and implemented unit recognition programs that awarded companies gold and silver streamers for excelling in physical fitness and marksmanship. These streamers were affixed to the top of the guidon, above the company flag.

A company needed at least 80% of its soldiers to qualify as experts on their M16A1 rifles to get the gold streamer. This was the easier streamer to keep. To be an infantry soldier, it was kind of a given that you had to be able to shoot a rifle and the inept were usually weeded out in basic training. Every soldier had to qualify with his weapon every six months, so there was always the risk of losing this streamer. But it was rare.

Then there was the silver streamer award for unit fitness. The minimum score to pass the Army Physical Fitness Test (APFT) was still sixty points in each of the three events; the pushup, sit-up and two-mile run. A company had to have an average score of eighty points in each event, which was not an easy task by any stretch of the imagination, to get the gold streamer. To make matters more difficult, no commander wanted the humiliation of not having this streamer on the company guidon. Every commander in the division over-prepared his company for the unit's Physical Training (PT) test.

By "over-prepared," I mean just that. Company PT sessions were still every Monday, Wednesday, and Friday and commanders pushed their soldiers as hard as they could during these sessions. Every company had a designated area where it conducted PT. The company would be placed in an extended rectangle formation and go through a series of exercises that challenged every muscle group, with an emphasis on pushups and sit-ups. We were then ordered back into a standard formation for the company run. I usually had to endure another session of pushups until my arms were like noodles and then sit-ups until I couldn't sit up at the completion of the morning run. As hard as this was, it was nothing compared to the grass drills.

Occasionally, we would finish a run back at our PT field expecting the usual muscle fatigue routine. Though I dreaded this, I knew it wouldn't last that long because I was already fatigued at this point. The company would come to a halt and we would be given the commands that put us in the extended formation for PT, but instead of calling out the order for pushups, the command "Go" would be given. I could actually hear every heart in the company sink as each one of us began running in place. "Go" was the start position for the dreaded grass drills.

Grass drills are difficult enough on their own, but to conduct them after a full PT session of exercising and running was pure torture. There are dozens of different exercises that can be done during grass drills to build strength and endurance, and sometimes I think they made some up just to inflict pain. The drills began in the "go" position, which was running in place. The commands for the different exercises would then be shouted out and I would have to move from one to the other as fast as I could and do the exercise, non-stop, until another command was given. Unlike routine exercising that was done to a cadence, grass drill required each exercise to be done at a rapid pace, without pause, until the next command.

The different commands and their respective exercises included the four basic ones: "go" was running in place, "front" was the prone, pushup position that required me to hold my body parallel to the ground with my chest six inches from the ground, "back" was lying on my back while holding my legs straight and six inches off the ground, and "stop" was a position like a football linebacker where I had to kind of squat, while leaning forward with one hand on the ground like I was getting ready to charge the quarterback.

There were basic exercises incorporated into the grass drill like pushups and sit-ups. Countless variations of the pushup: hands wide, farther out than the standard shoulder width apart; and narrow, which was hands close together, palms down and index fingers and thumbs touching. I can't leave out the bouncing hand clap pushups which required thrusting my torso up in the air, clapping my hands, and then landing back in the upright pushup position. Of course, this could also be done from each of the different pushup hand positions. There were flutter kicks, leg scissors, rolls right and left, side benders, knee benders, and on and on. All of this was designed to get me conditioned to score high on the big semi-annual PT tests. On Tuesdays and Thursdays, we formed up by platoon for our morning PT sessions, which was more of the same but not as extreme. I looked forward to these days.

I don't want to take away from the running though. Those morning runs were by far the hardest part of PT for me. Schofield Barracks was a pretty big base so there were plenty of directions for us to run five or six miles without repeating any route. This may have helped break up the monotony at the beginning of the run but after the first couple of miles, most eyes were either on the ground watching your feet or staring straight ahead at the head in front of you. Running on asphalt, in formation, at a pace designed to challenge you was very painful. I have long legs and running in formation required a shorter step to stay in line with the others in your row and not tangle feet with the guy in front of you. The one thing that helped me with the runs is I always volunteered to lead the formation. This allowed me to run beside the formation and take my more natural stride.

Leading the formation required singing the cadence that was used to keep the formation in step. There are countless different songs and lyrics but I always had my favorites that I sang. They were my favorites because I thought I sounded good singing them. I never thought to ask for a second opinion. I had to concentrate to keep the appropriate beat without gasping for air which kept me from thinking about the pain my body was experiencing. I think it provided a distraction for everyone. The last mile or so was always done at a faster pace; this made cadence impossible to sing. By this point I just tried to keep some sort of order to the exhausted formation by hollering out a cadence of, "one, two, three, four, left, right, left."

Most mornings, our route took us through the family housing area. Running with large apartment buildings on both sides of the road amplified the singing significantly. It was cool hearing the volume increase and the slight echo this created. Military families were used to the sound of unit after unit running by their apartments early every morning. When they had family visiting, as we all did on occasion, I am sure it was a bit of a shock hearing this every morning.

My mom flew my grandmother, my little brother James, and little sister Amy out to spend a month with me during their summer break. One morning, like so many other mornings, I was singing the cadence as my company was running through the housing area where I lived. As we approached the rear of my apartment, I could see my grandmother sitting on the patio in her pajamas and smoking a cigarette. When we were close enough, I waved so she would see me leading the formation. What I didn't expect was for her to stand up and point at me yelling loudly, "Hey it's Bobby! Look its Bobby! Hi Bobby!" Uh, oh. This wasn't going to end well for me. For a long time after this, everyone in my chain of command took pleasure in calling me Bobby. The whole scene was very embarrassing back then but what a great memory of my grandmother I have now.

Then there were the payday runs. These were the most excruciating runs I ever participated in and I had to go through this grueling task on every end-of-the-month payday. It was a division run that was spectacular to witness. Row after row of soldiers, company after company, running in step and singing different cadence that echoed off the barracks walls as we ran through the streets of the base towards the Kolekole Pass. Once we exited the housing area, we turned onto Trimble Road and the buildings became sparse as the road started its ascent, continually turning left and right in its steady upward slant. There was a guarded gate at the summit of the pass where we turned around and headed back. If you ran the direct route up to the gate and then back to your company area it was over eight miles. Some battalion commanders like to exert their control and ran their units longer distances so it wasn't uncommon to sometimes make a loop around base before ending the pain.

The knowledge that my paycheck was hitting my bank account this day took a little of the sting out of this monthly run. Very little. Nothing could take away the screaming sore muscles, fatigue, and occasional blistered feet these runs inflicted on me. I am sure that more than a few are like me, paying a price in my older age from the continuous strains my body was put through pounding the pavement up and down that pass.

Since I was in a grunt unit, I had to keep physically prepared for the possibility of a long-distance combat road march. A timed, twelve-mile forced march in full combat gear was occasionally scheduled to insure the unit's ability to complete it in the expert infantryman requirement of three hours or less. The farthest road march I ever completed in full combat gear was twenty-five miles. I had to go on a twenty-five-mile forced march on the rough, hilly terrain just outside the post right after arriving in Hawaii. I don't even know how to describe the difficulty of this mind-numbing trek. I just know I am thankful I never had to do this again.

I did go on countless combat road marches in full gear. There wasn't any specific time limit for most of them, with the only objective that we all finish together as a unit. Normally, these road marches were schedule when I was deployed to a training area where I would

116

march from camp to the training sites and then back at the end of the day.

Whenever my unit deployed for an extended period, there would be a full day scheduled for one long road march. Hoofing it along the paved and dirt roads of the training area all day with no end in sight was an extremely difficult task for the mind and body. Feet screaming, sweat pouring down my face, I had to trek on with no idea when it would end. These marches were done in a staggered formation with guys alternating an equal distance apart on each side of the road. Rifles were pointed outward, away from the road with everyone constantly searching for movement. Each soldier had a responsibility for a ten-meter area on his side of the road, continually scanning it for an enemy attack. When someone slowed down, a gap was created and enemy movement could be missed.

Being in a leadership position, I would walk the center of the road trying to keep everyone motivated. Leading a road march is nothing like leading a running formation. In road marches, I always had to walk up and down the formation to ensure the proper intervals were kept. The security of the unit could depend on this. It was the responsibility of the unit leaders to make sure this was maintained the entire time of the road march. This constant roaming up and down the formation meant I always traveled much farther than my soldiers by the end of the march. This training was about building endurance which is why distance was never revealed and there were no time limits.

I did get breaks, stopping at specific intervals for short periods to check my feet for blisters, change socks, and refill my canteens. Hydration in the Hawaiian heat was very important so a deuce-and-a-half (2-1/2) ton truck would follow the formation pulling a water tank known as a water buffalo. This provided a constant source of water at each break to fill up canteens, dampen bandanas, or just pour over my head. Everyone did these tasks as fast as possible so that most of the break time could be spent semi-conscious in the shade. As a leader, I got my rest in smaller intervals because I had to make sure no one spent the entire time comatose, neglecting the important tasks. My first priority was the welfare of my men by making sure everyone had taken care of their feet and hydration. The adage "No rest for the weary" was never more true to me than during these marches. Many of these road marches were scheduled by me during my time as Training NCO so I only had myself to blame for having to endure them.

I finally got the opportunity in 1985 to qualify for the Army Expert Infantryman Badge (EIB). On my list of awards that I wanted during my career, the EIB ranked towards the top, right under Meritorious Service Medal. I had to successfully complete a rigorous series of tests over several consecutive days to earn this award. These tests were designed to prove my expertise at being an infantry soldier. I first had to have an expert qualification with the M16A1 rifle to even be eligible for this testing. Since I was also an anti-armor infantryman, I had to have an expert qualification with the TOW system as well. I had to successfully complete a day and night land navigation course, a twelve-mile road march in full combat gear including weapon and a thirty-five-pound ruck sack in under three hours, and pass the standard physical fitness test of push-ups, sit-ups, and two-mile run.

I had to go through a round-robin set up with thirty to forty stations that tested my knowledge in different infantry skills. There were stations for different types of first aid techniques like CPR, treating broken bones, burns, and open chest wounds. I was tested on assembling and disassembling various hand held weapons and the proper firing techniques for each one. I had to be able to identify different mines, American and Soviet, and clear an enemy mine field. I was tested on communication skills, including hand signals, the phonetic alphabet, radio procedures, and the proper way for calling for indirect fire support. There were stations that tested my nuclear, biological, and chemical knowledge and proficiency as well.

At each station, I was given a "go" or "no go." I had to receive a go at all the stations to qualify for the EIB. I could receive a no go on three stations or less and be allowed a second attempt at those stations. A "no go" on more than three stations and I would have failed to qualify.

I was one of the few fortunate ones who passed all the requirements and qualified for the Expert Infantry Badge. I proudly wore it for the remainder of my career.

Chapter 19
NCO of the Year

I had the honor and pleasure of being selected by my chain of command to represent my company in the competition for the battalion NCO of the 3rd Quarter of 1986. This was much more difficult than the process I went through in Germany at the beginning of my career. There were a bunch of subjects in leadership and general categories that I had to be knowledgeable in. These topics included leadership skill and traits, NCO duties and responsibilities, weapons, drill and ceremony, unit history, chain of command, physical training, Geneva convention, NBC (nuclear, biological, and chemical warfare), code of conduct, first aid, military justice, guard duty, flags, and current events. Not only did I have to know these subjects, I had to know which army regulations or field manuals covered them.

This required lots of study time. My platoon sergeant gave me some down time to prepare for this but most of the preparation was done during my evenings at home. I spent every spare moment reading manuals and memorizing everything I could to prepare myself. The soldiers in my section would occasionally quiz me on some of these things when they weren't teasing me. I watched lots of news every day to keep up with current events. Thank God CNN had introduced the Headline News channel that covered just the headlines and every thirty minutes started over. I would keep the TV on this channel whenever I was studying. You hear the same news being covered every half hour, you can't help but remember it.

I easily won the battalion process and was selected to compete against the other battalion winners for the brigade NCO of the Quarter honor. I knew this was going to be a more difficult challenge competing against a higher caliber of NCO's who had proven their expertise and were the best of their battalions.

I was exempted from training the days leading up to the competition to focus on this challenge. By this time, it was a big deal to everyone in my platoon and my company that I win so I found much more support and assistance while I prepared. I appreciated all the help even though I still took a lot of ribbing from them. I soon found myself even more up to speed on all the topics and was more than ready to face the challenge when it finally came.

The board was led by the brigade command sergeant major (CSM) and made up of five senior NCO's, including the CSM's over each battalion in the brigade. Facing these powerful men whom I had been conditioned to both fear and respect was the most challenging part of the competition. Nervous as I was, I knew my material and breezed through the questions each of them asked and came away as the winner and with the honor of being Brigade NCO of the 3rd Quarter of 1986. I was awarded a plaque to commemorate this achievement and an Army Achievement Medal.

The year came to an end and I learned I wasn't finished with these competitions. I was informed I had to go back in front of the board once again for the Brigade NCO of the Year award. This time I would face even tougher competition going against the winners of the other three quarters. I buried myself once again in army regulations while listening to an endless thirty-minute loop of Headline News. I read and reread army manuals and standards until I felt like I had them memorized forward and backwards. I had guys in my unit quizzing me when I grew tired of reading. I stuck to this routine right up until I was scheduled to report to the board. My first sergeant seemed to want the recognition of having this award won by one of his NCO's pretty badly. He gave me all the time I needed to prepare. He also assigned categories to each platoon sergeant in the company and convened a mock board to prepare me. They grilled me with questions for hours and hours until my answers seemed to flow out without any signs of nervousness or uncertainty. The day finally came and I once again found myself facing the brigade board but this time I didn't feel any of the intimidation that had overwhelmed me before. All the preparation paid off and I won this round of competition and the prestigious title of Brigade NCO of the Year for 1986. I received another plaque and Army Achievement Medal for this accomplishment.

Immediately after winning the brigade competition, I found myself competing for the 25th Infantry Division NCO of the Year, facing off against all the different brigade winners. I went over all the material once again before facing the division board. Not much time had passed since the brigade board so all the information was still fresh in my mind. To say I was nervous wouldn't come close to what it felt like this time. The board was led by the division Command Sergeant Major, the highest ranking enlisted man in the division. The rest of the board consisted of the CSM's over each brigade in the division, including mine, whose presence instantly comforted me. He still intimidated the heck out of me, but it was reassuring seeing him when I entered the room.

Unfortunately, I didn't win the division competition but was runner up to the winner from the 3rd Brigade. I was awarded a handshake from the division CSM for reaching this level. Surprisingly, being in the same room with the most powerful NCO's at the top of my chain of command, leaders who under different circumstances wouldn't have given me a second glance, proved to be very rewarding in itself.

Chapter 20
BNCOC
Basic Non-Commissioned
Officers Course

As an E-5 Sergeant, the army required me to attend the basic non-commissioned officers course (BNCOC). This was the next level of NCO training to prepare me to be in charge of a platoon. Just like PLDC at Fort Knox, I was required to reside on-site for the duration of the course. The class was held on the side of a mountain on the northeast part of the island. I rode a bus that traveled up a winding, paved road into a wooded area in the middle of nowhere from Schofield Barracks. The school was enclosed by a fence with barbed wire on top and was completely isolated from any signs of civilization. The only structure nearby was a huge wind farm with its giant wind mills that were constantly spinning from the island winds. The compound itself was nothing more than a small, older building divided into three sections: a sleeping area on one end, a small classroom in the middle, and a cafeteria on the other end.

This school was specifically for infantry non-commissioned officers so the curriculum focused on leadership in an infantry unit. The size of the class was small and only required two instructors. Staff Sergeant Bullard did most of our instruction and was onsite every day and most nights. He had recently been in a Ranger unit that was involved in the very short invasion of Grenada that ousted the communist regime and restored democracy to the island. There was a second instructor who assisted when needed.

Being confined to the compound, I endured twelve to fifteen hours of lessons each day. Because my class was so small, we quickly knitted into a tight group that proved to be beneficial to all of us. We were able to work closely together insuring that everyone graduated. I was tested and given a pass or fail grade for every lesson that was taught. I had to pass every subject or I would have failed the course and been sent back to my unit with my tail between my legs.

I was still in the infantry and part of a division focused on fitness, so PT was conducted daily. Of all the strenuous activities, I endured in my career, the PT sessions at BNCOC were some of the most demanding. The payday runs up the Kolekole Pass were by far the hardest and the longest, going mostly uphill one way and downhill the other. Since the school was located halfway up a mountain, the surrounding roads wound up and down along the ridges. I ran every single one of those roads, up and down, up and down, winding around that mountain. The inclines were much steeper and harder on my legs than I was used to. As I ran these tortuous routes, I always seemed to be waiting for the instructor to call for the turnaround so the formation could begin working its way back to the compound.

I got to know every one of those winding roads closely, every intersection and fork, and where each direction would take me. Every crossroad led to more hills and more pain, just different levels of it. I quickly learned which routes offered the least punishment. Short of breath, face red and dripping with sweat, I approached each intersection filled with trepidation, never knowing what direction I would go. I closed in on these crossroads overcome with dread, praying for the turnaround order that never seemed to be given. One foot in front of the other, on to the next intersection with the same hope and the same dread.

SSG Bullard had a sick sense of humor and played on this suffering every morning. He would give the order taking the class down the road offering the easier terrain. We would run a short distance and then be turned around and led down the harder road. Pure mind games. Other times, we would reach what we thought was the halfway point and turn around only to be taken a short distance and turned back around. It was pure torture running up and down that terrain as it was and yet we had to endure these mind games during every run. Like everything I did in the infantry, this was no different and I was pushed further and further as my endurance improved. For every route that was conquered there was always another one to be tackled so it never got easier the entire time I was there.

The unique terrain that surrounded the school allowed for some advanced land navigation training. I spent a considerable amount of time roaming the area learning to read and navigate the steep, wooded terrain.

Being a small, secured facility provided an excellent opportunity to train on different security procedures. For example, I had to come up with a security plan to prevent a breach of the facility by an enemy. I had to devise a rescue mission to gain access to the facility and secure an imaginary prisoner, which required planning and executing a reconnaissance mission to familiarize myself with the compound and surrounding area. I applied camouflage makeup to my face and moved in and out of various positions overlooking the school. From these stealth positions, I drew a map with as much detail as I could in the allotted time and withdrew a safe distance to develop a plan to get in, secure the prisoner, and retreat to the designated base camp. This kind of training was the cool part of the academy, giving me a short reprieve from the physical demands of the morning PT and the hours listening to lectures in the classroom. I loved hands-on activities like this that allowed me to be creative. I suspect it was also because it reminded me of those bygone days from my youth, playing army with my buddies and letting my imagination run wild.

Eventually the course ended and there was a fancy graduation ceremony. Sitting in my assigned seat, like I had done every day that past month, in the air-conditioned classroom, SSG Bullard handed me my diploma and the designated NCO ribbon and medal to be worn on my dress uniform. He then announced the Honor Graduate for the course. I was surprised and proud to learn that he had bestowed this honor on me. For this accomplishment, I was awarded another Army Achievement Medal.

Chapter 21
Company Training NCO

Soon after my first year in Hawaii, I was asked to take over the open Training NCO position and I jumped at the chance. 1SG Anderson, for whom I had a tremendous amount of respect, had recommended me to the company commander for this position. I was reassigned to the headquarters platoon, and as the highest-ranking person, I was assigned the responsibility of platoon sergeant as well. This put me in charge of the supply room, company armor, and the front office in addition to my duties as Training NCO. 1SG Anderson was soon reassigned to a company in another battalion and tried in vain to get approval for me to be reassigned with him. By this time, I think I had proven to be a valuable asset for Captain Gillette because he refused to approve this transfer.

This was a position I felt I was born to do. As the Training NCO, I was responsible for planning and scheduling the training for my entire company, my former anti-tank platoon, the mortar platoon, and the reconnaissance, also known as the scout platoon. I reported directly to the company commander and worked with the respective platoon leaders to schedule and coordinate whatever they requested for training their guys. I then worked closely with each platoon sergeant for the implementation and execution of this training.

I worked for Captain Ronald Gillette when I first took over the position. He was later replaced by Captain Samuel Young. I was their assigned driver so I spent lots of time with these guys and became very close to them. Captain Gillette and I had a more formal relationship, maintaining a high regard and respect for each other. Captain Young and I had developed a much closer bond and friendship that sometimes crossed the commander/subordinate lines. I always felt like we were as close to tight friends as military protocol would allow. Both taught me valuable lessons about how to fulfill my responsibilities to the people under my command. I also became quite close with Lieutenant John Lambert, the company executive officer for most of my time as training NCO. There were several times he was very helpful in coordinating some of the more creative training I scheduled.

My desk was in the front office that I shared with the company clerk, Marlon Brose, who primarily worked for the First Sergeant. The front office was centrally located with the offices of the first sergeant, company commander, and executive officer surrounding us. The five of us who filled these positions always worked very well together resulting in the smoothest running front office in the battalion. At the risk of sounding arrogant, I have no doubt we were the best trained infantry company in the division.

I took on this position full throttle and poured everything I had into it. I came in every morning at 4:30 am to have some alone time to prepare for the day's activities. First formation of the day was for reveille at 6:30 am, so I had plenty of time to review the day's training schedule for each platoon and insure all the logistics were taken care of. This quiet time provided me a chance to complete most of my paperwork for the day, whether it be typing correspondences for the commander, filling out requisition forms for supplies, or filing the gazillion different reports and records I was responsible for maintaining. By getting everything done early in the morning, I would be available the rest of the day for whatever the company commander might require from me. When the time came to form up outside for reveille, I would take charge of my platoon as we marched over to the PT field and endured that morning's grueling workout and run. At the conclusion, the front office staff usually met informally for some extra pushups and sit-ups before showering and reporting back for the 9:00 am formation.

I no longer participated in platoon-level training but there was plenty to keep me busy. For one thing, I had my own platoon to worry about and the responsibility of the company's weapon and supply needs. Most my time was spent working on future training schedules which involved more than thinking of something and placing it on a training calendar. Firing ranges and training sites had to be coordinated and approved in advance. If there was a specific support item one of the platoon leaders or the company commander needed, I had to track it down and go through the procedures to procure it by the date it was needed. Because of my good relationships with each platoon leader, I knew most of their training needs so they gave me complete autonomy to schedule for them.

I always attempted to spend time with each platoon in my company when they were out training. If they were away for an extended training session, I tried to spend at least one night with them. I believed good leadership was not done from the shadows or in the background. Leading by example and doing things right beside the people you are responsible for is true leadership. I was responsible for every platoon when it came to training and I took this very seriously. It is the little things like this that keep your soldiers motivated and excited about the training they are involved in. Only weak leaders stay behind their desks while their soldiers are enduring challenging training.

There were training requirements for each platoon that had to be scheduled regularly so that each soldier could maintain proficiency in his job. I liked to schedule training that spiced these things up and exposed the guys to new challenges. I always tried to give them new experiences that would make them better soldiers, not only for us but for the remainder of their military careers.

As infantry soldiers, we needed to be trained in basic forms of survival skills. Being the guys on the front line, we had to be prepared for the possibility of getting separated from our unit and having to survive on our own. It's hard to learn something and retain that knowledge sitting in a classroom. Hands-on training was the best way to learn new skills and remember that knowledge.

One time the XO and I thought it would be great to teach advanced survival skills. The platoons were out for a few days of live fire exercises when I scheduled the day to end earlier than normal to conduct this training. The first part of the class was spent teaching these soldiers how to find food in the environment around them. The XO conducted the training, showing everyone the more common safe foods that could be found in nature as well as what things to stay away from. Next, they were given instruction on different ways for starting a fire with sticks to cook a meal. Lastly, a live chicken was given to each squad and they were taught how to humanely kill it, prepare it, and cook it over an open fire. Their dinner meal that evening had to be prepared by each squad using the skills they had just learned.

With the help of the Lieutenant Lambert, I was able to procure live chickens for this training. This was not an easy task in Hawaii. First I had to get permission from the Division S-3 and had to request the funds to pay for them through the finance office. Then a source for the chickens had to be found locally. Fortunately, the XO finally found them. The chickens were picked up the afternoon of the training and delivered in time for the evening lesson. A lot of effort went into pulling this off.

We researched different ways to kill a chicken because we didn't want the company to have to do it old fashioned way by grabbing the bird and breaking its neck. The XO found a way to hypnotize the chicken so the squads could kill it with an axe to the neck without having to hold it still. Hypnotizing chickens was surprisingly simple and seemed humane. One person had to hold the chicken with its belly on the ground and one hand on the top of its neck, forcing the chicken to look straight ahead. Once the chicken was secured, another person had to take a stick and place one end down in the dirt in front of the bird's beak. A line was then drawn in the ground with the stick, repeatedly pulling the stick away from the chicken in a very slow, deliberate line. Over and over the stick was slowly pulled away from his beak until the chicken became completely still, hypnotized by the motion of the stick. This is very similar to how the lines going down the center of a road can make a driver start nodding off. Once the chicken was hypnotized, it no longer needed to be held down. It just laid there staring straight ahead while someone grabbed an axe and finished the job. I am confident that every guy who went through this training remembers it to this day. Not just the gory part, but every aspect of the training they got that day.

I would schedule training away from Schofield Barracks occasionally to give the guys a break. On the northeast side of the island was an area known as Bellows Air Force Station. It bordered the ocean and had great waves most of the time. I had spent many weekends there with my family in rented cabins or just spending the day picnicking and boogie boarding with the kids. I knew this would be an awesome beach to train on.

I scheduled a short trip there for the company. For the training, we practiced the procedures for conducting a beach assault and defending from a beach assault. I also contacted the Air Force and got them to provide a chinook helicopter for helocast training. This involved jumping from the chinook while it hovered close to the ocean. This took their training to a whole new level. Not to mention that *anything* done on a beach is awesome anyway.

I was also responsible for scheduling and maintaining the records for the PT tests and the weapons qualification tests. With the division guidon streamer status on the line, I had to insure they were scheduled and completed before the deadline of six months from the last qualification or we would lose the streamer, something I did not want to happen. This responsibility included testing the battalion staff as well, including the battalion commander.

Typically, the run portion of the PT test was conducted on a track just like used in running competitions. The track was a quarter of a mile in length and two miles was eight laps around the track. I hated running laps on a track with a vengeance because it made the run as much psychological as it was physical. I decided to change this by scheduling the run around the perimeter of our PT field.

I took the commander's Jeep out and marked a route of two miles from start to finish for the company to run for one of these PT tests. Standing at the end of the route with a stop watch, I would call out the times as each person passed. The times were quickly written down to be recorded on their PT test forms. The times were unbelievable with everyone finishing in personal best times leading me to think I was a genius for trying this continuous two-mile route. This moment would pass rather quickly when my company commander informed me that the battalion commander didn't believe his new time was accurate. I was asked to review the distance again. To my utter shock and embarrassment, I had marked the route two tenths of a mile shy of two miles. No wonder the times were so good. How was I going to tell my commander and what would the battalion commander do to me for this blunder?

I was sick with worry as I confessed this blunder to my boss. To my utter shock, he laughed and told me I had to tell the battalion commander myself. Feeling like I could throw up any minute I slowly climbed the stairs to the battalion offices with all kinds of scenarios going through my mind. None of them good. After knocking and entering his office, fully expecting the worst, which by this time was really bad in my mind, I was again surprised when he simply said, "Reschedule it, Kern, and try to get the distance right this time." Knowing I had just dodged a huge bullet, I decided the re-test would be conducted running laps on the base track where everyone knew exactly how many laps it took to complete two miles. No harm, no foul it seemed. I later learned my blunder was brought up at the next commanders' meeting and they all had a good laugh at my expense.

Every quarter we had to go through battalion inspections that were designed to make sure we were always combat ready. I always thought it was just another excuse for someone in a command position to flex his muscle. The equipment had to be laid out precisely the same as specified in the battalion standards of operation for inspections. This inspection was conducted by the battalion staff. Vehicles were inspected in the motor pool with every weapon system assembled to the rear of the vehicle. This battalion commander wasn't as anal as the one I had in Germany so there was no sign of a white glove in the motor pool. There were weapons formations to inspect our rifles and uniforms. And, of course, there was the training room inspection.

Training room inspections were much more in-depth because everything had to meet the military standards laid out in the many different army regulations. These were mostly administrative inspections and covered all the paperwork required by the army, like individual records for PT tests and weapons qualification. One by one, these documents were inspected to verify dates, scores, signature of the NCO and the officer who were present to witness it and, of course, my signature to verify the testing was done by military standards. Part of my job required me to maintain a library of training manuals for the unit. This was checked to insure I had a copy of every manual that could be used by an infantry headquarters company. The theory behind this was that there should always be a copy of every manual on hand in the event someone in the unit needed to verify a procedure or standard. In my entire time in this position, I never had one person approach me to look up something from one of these manuals. I can't help but think about all the companies in my battalion, my brigade, and my division, and then the hundreds of companies overall in the military that were maintaining these same libraries in their training rooms. That's a lot of money in manuals and typical government waste. The big news in the civilian world at this time was the overspending of the government, particularly the military. News stations were talking about the army's famous $250 toilet seats and $100 hammers but I don't ever recall hearing stories about these training room stockpiles of manuals. Nevertheless, every aspect of a training room was inspected and scored with points deducted for each discrepancy and missing item.

As I mentioned previously, this time in my career I had become somewhat of a perfectionist and took pride in everything I did no matter how small it seemed. My training room was no exception. I would accept nothing less than the highest score and always worked to accomplish this. There was also a carrot dangled when these inspections started. The Training NCO with the best score would be awarded an Army Achievement Medal. I got the highest score in the battalion and the AAM awarded to me the first time I went through this process. In fact, I got the highest score every quarter, but the battalion commander wouldn't award more than one AAM to a soldier for these quarterly inspections. Yes, it ticked me off, but neither my performance nor my attitude were affected, nor was my drive to do the best I could.

I also wanted my platoons to be the best that they could be. I went to great lengths to be creative when scheduling company and platoon training. I made countless trips upstairs to my battalion Staff-3 (S-3) and frequent runs to the division headquarters and S-3 offices to find available dates and reserve sites for my unit. I developed relationships with my brigade and division training staffs that helped me fulfill any training requests the platoon leaders and sergeants wanted.

I knew training couldn't always be regimented and the guys needed time scheduled for fun. No matter who my company commander and first sergeant were, I always tried to keep the unit lightened up with events that had nothing to do with training. One such event was a talent contest. We set a date for this and would insert times in the training schedule for the guys to work on whatever talent or skit they wanted to do. The things the guys came up with were outrageous including parodies of the commanders and other funny skits. It was hilarious! The first sergeant, company commander and I acted as the judges but all we did was stand to the side and laugh uncontrollably.

As each skit was performed, the guys made it clear they wanted the front office to do a skit. We finally succumbed to the pressure and huddled to come up with something that we could do. Break dancing was very popular at the time so we decided to perform a skit which had the first sergeant and Captain Young attempting to dance to rap music while I laid on my back with my feet in the air. They would dance around me, taking turns grabbing my feet, and spinning me in a circle. I would assume some sort of break dancing pose as my spinning slowed, only to be spun again before I stopped. We tried to do this with some sort of tempo to no avail. None of us had a single ounce of rhythm, so we looked ridiculous with our attempts to break dance. The guys were all close to tears laughing at us up there, which was exactly what we wanted. I have no idea who won the talent contest that day but I know I sure felt like a winner. I bet every single person in our company that day can remember our misguided attempt at break dancing. I know I do.

The best award I ever got as Training NCO came the day of the change of command for my company commanders. Both of them spent time visiting in the commander's office. Captain Gillette was giving Captain Young a heads-up about the company and the men, to ease the transition. After the change of command ceremony, I was visiting with Captain Young and he shared with me the discussions they had. He told me that Captain Gillette had said that it was a pretty easy job as company commander because Staff Sergeant Kern was the one who really ran the company. Not true but it felt very good to learn he had so much faith in me.

Chapter 22
Cobra Gold 86

The first long term deployment I went on as the company Training NCO was to Thailand in 1986 when my unit participated in the second annual Cobra Gold exercise. Forty-five days in the hot, humid jungles to participate in this multinational exercise designed to show our support to the small countries in Southeast Asia. The exercise allowed soldiers to get acclimated to this type of warfare while cross training with foreign military units. As was common during the Cold War Era, it was also a show of force to discourage communist regimes, particularly Vietnam, of any thoughts of attacking these countries. The Vietnam War, which had ended badly eleven years earlier, made it vitally important to show that we stood behind Thailand and its neighbors.

Preparation for this was a little different than for other deployments. I was used to training in the tropical climate of Hawaii but I had no idea how much more difficult training would be in the dense jungles. I had to schedule mandatory classes that were conducted by the battalion staff officers and medics to prepare everyone for this deployment. Everyone needed to learn how to identify the different poisonous snakes and wild life that could be encountered (such as scorpions, which were very common.) Even though they weren't deadly, their sting was quite painful so they needed to be avoided like a bee or wasp is. This meant opening and shaking your boots thoroughly before putting them on and checking your sleeping bag from top to bottom before jumping in. The temperature and humidity was also going to be a concern so we went over the symptoms of heat stroke and heat exhaustion and the preventative measures for these conditions.

I had to get shots and take tons of pills to prevent malaria, dengue fever, and other diseases common to this country. Passports had to be acquired. Additional gear was issued that was necessary for jungle training. A mosquito net had to be draped over my cot at night to keep the huge mosquitos from carrying me away in my sleep. I was issued an aluminum support frame that attached to my cot that the net could be secured to. When we breathe, our bodies absorb the oxygen and what is exhaled is full of carbon dioxide. I had heard somewhere that mosquitoes can detect this carbon dioxide and are attracted by it. This makes sense because during this deployment, I had to wear a mosquito net that hung from the front of my helmet to keep them from attacking my face and neck.

Everything had to be loaded into the C-5 planes that we would travel in. The C-5's were large planes used to transport soldiers and their equipment. Because of their size, the wings had to be huge. They were so long they dipped down and almost touched the ground. Commercial airline seats were installed in the front of the cargo area for the soldiers to sit. The Jeeps and equipment were strapped down behind the seats in the rear of the plane and in the lower deck. The flight was extremely long taking fifteen or so hours mostly over water. There was a quick stop in Guam where I could get off the plane and stretch my legs. The flight was so long, they had to refuel the plane while it was in the air. My seat may have been a commercial airline seat, lap tray and all, but that was the only thing this flight had in common with a commercial one.

There were no MP3's back then, or anything else to really distract me during this flight. Most of the time I slept, but the flight was so long it was impossible to sleep the entire time. I was prepared though and had brought lots of books to pass the time. But no matter what I did to fill the hours, cabin fever eventually affected me. There were no stewardesses to bring drinks or packs of peanuts, so a hot meal was not an option. Meals were served by someone throwing me an MRE. I was miserable by the time I landed in Thailand. I have never been so glad to feel solid ground under my feet, even if the temperature felt like it was a gazillion degrees outside.

We traveled to a military base in the province of Chonburi where I was housed in bamboo barracks. No air conditioning or even windows to open. It was so hot that windows wouldn't have made a difference anyway. Thank God I had already grown accustomed to sleeping in any climate no matter how severe. I was housed in a smaller building with CPT Gillette, the XO, and his driver. When I got there, I quickly staked out a corner where I assembled my cot and mosquito net. On the opposite end of the billet area, just a short walk away, was a shower building which proved to be a very important comfort after spending a day in the jungle.

I loved my job as training NCO but never as much as I did during this deployment. The training schedule was primarily handled at the division and brigade level so my main responsibility during this trip was driving the commander. No walking, running or training whatsoever, just driving him wherever he needed to be. There were so many perks during this trip I still get excited just thinking about the experience I had there.

Most of the company training was conducted in the jungle. There were tiny dirt roads, more like paths, that allowed me to get my Jeep to every training site. While navigating these paths in my Jeep, I would come across these little eateries at random locations. They were not fancy places, just big hut-like building with no walls. Each one was the same and featured a large wok in the center of the structure on a table. Around this was a narrow countertop in the shape of a square and a wooden bench for the customers to sit at that went around the perimeter and faced the wok. Separating the table and wok was a narrow pathway barely large enough for one person to walk around the wok to cook and serve. They all had only one item they offered, a dish called Khao Phat. This was a fried rice dish with onions and other vegetables that they would stir fry while you waited. Right before it was done they cracked a few eggs and threw them in the wok to cook to finish it off. Throw a little of their red-hot sauce on it and, man oh man, it was unbelievable. Every time we passed one of these "diners" in the jungles we had a short debate about whether we had time to stop or not. I tried in vain for years to find this dish with no success. I thought it was called Cow Pot and whenever I would find a Thai restaurant stateside, I would ask if they served Cow Pot. They would look at me like I was an idiot. Turns out I am and I bet the servers in Thailand thought the same thing. I wouldn't be surprised if they still laugh when they remember that idiot American GI who always ordered Cow Pot.

Back at base camp someone had found a house a short trip up a trail from where our mess hall was set up. The folks who lived there made this Khao Phat and sold it from their back door. Every chance I had, I would sneak down the trail and buy it. It wasn't uncommon to see a line of soldiers formed at their back door. Like all good secrets this one reached the ears of higher ups and the place was banned from our use. No reason was ever given so it was another instance of someone in power flexing his authority to remind us who was in charge. It was a stupid ban and a few of us still sneaked back there a time or two more.

Part of the Cobra Gold exercise was going through a round-robin of stations to learn about jungle warfare. The most popular of these stations was the one that covered jungle survival. One day while checking on training, Captain Gillette and I stopped to watch the demonstration given by a Thai soldier. The first part involved techniques to procure water and avoid dehydration in the jungle heat. He gave a demonstration on the extreme measures you could take if necessary to survive. Drinking your own pee was the extreme measure, the most extreme in my opinion, and he actually peed in a plastic bag and drank it. Disgusting, but something I will never forget.

Next he showed us the different types of snakes that could be found in Southeast Asia. He had them stored in wooden crates and as he opened each box he would pick up the venomous snake to show us up close what it looked like. He then passed around plastic bags of smoked rattlesnake to be sampled if you wanted. I tried a small piece and wasn't impressed. The smoking of the meat overwhelmed the taste and it was slightly greasy. It tasted nothing like chicken, although to be fair I have never tried smoked chicken.

He closed out his demonstration with the King Cobra. This was both terrifying and awesome. Two guys carried out this large wooden crate and unlatched it. The crate lid was thrown back and when the snake didn't appear he rapped the box with his stick. At this time, a huge cobra shot straight up and I swear it stared the guy straight in the eye. I know Thai folks are shorter in stature than us but this was still an amazing sight to see. The instructor then started circling the snake, tapping it on the back of the head to get it down so he could grab it. As the suspense and terror was building, Captain Gillette quickly approached and said it was time to go. From the pale look on his face, and the terror in his eyes, I never considered questioning this command. We jumped in the Jeep and headed back to camp in silence. But that was fine with me. Some things far outweigh our personal interests.

The command and support units for the division were located at an abandoned airstrip that had been used during the Vietnam War. I spent a lot of time here while Captain Gillette attended daily meetings and briefings. I typically found a quiet corner and read one of the many books I had brought. I read a lot of science fiction and westerns. This is where I got to know many of the brigade and division staff which would become a great resource for me when I returned to Schofield Barracks. I got to hang out with some of the helicopter pilots which was really cool. I didn't know this at the time but they were required to log a specific number of hours flying each week. One day when I was there for one of the longer briefings, I was approached by one of the HUEY pilots and invited to ride along with him while he logged some flight time. I jumped at this opportunity.

The flight was one of the most awesome things I have ever done in my life. I believe there were three helicopters counting the one I was in. They flew in combat formation, hugging the tree lines. Up and down, right and left they flew, using the terrain as camouflage to cover our flight. They slowed whenever they came upon key landmarks and the pilot switched to tour guide mode telling me what we were approaching while giving me plenty of time to take it all in. Then he sped up and more combat flying techniques were practiced until we came upon another key point. Our flight took us near the Big Buddha statue, painted a shiny gold and so big you could see it from far away. It was an amazing thing to see something so iconic from this perspective. Simply amazing! Eventually, the helicopter turned around to head back to the airfield. Before I knew it, my exhilarating first and only flight in a HUEY was over.

Chapter 23
Light Infantry

The military has always evolved as the threats against our country and allies changed. Once we had shaken off the chains of the Vietnam War, this evolution was fast. We first upgraded our armored units in both size and technology. This was at the height of the Cold War and the biggest threat the world faced then was the Soviet Union and the Warsaw Pact. We knew the general geographical areas that we might have to defend and we prepared accordingly.

Towards the end of 1986, the 25th Infantry Division converted to a light infantry division. The threat of the Soviets was diminishing and the Army realized the threat was now more likely to come from other smaller hotspots around the world. Heavy armored divisions were big and bulky and would take too much time to deploy to one of these hotspots quickly. The powers that be at the very top of the chain of command decided, rightly so, that the military needed smaller, lighter units that could quickly deploy wherever needed. They wanted the versatility to send these lighter units quickly to more than one location if needed. The 25th Infantry Division was one of the first to be converted to light infantry. We were still responsible for threats in the Pacific Basin with communism still strong in Vietnam and North Korea.

In my brigade, a third battalion was added as part of this transition. In 1987, our antique Jeeps were replaced by the newly introduced High Mobility Multipurpose Wheeled Vehicle (HMMWV). Since my company had the anti-armor, reconnaissance and mortar platoons, we received three different configured Humvees with the appropriate armament for each platoon. This required each platoon to go through an intense training period to quickly learn the new combat procedures for their Humvees.

Towards the end of that year, my last year in the army, a small contingent of guys from my unit were selected to attend a light infantry course on the mainland and get certified as light infantry instructors for this. They returned to the company and were responsible for training and certifying the rest of the unit.

I was certain we were already fit enough for this new role as a light infantry soldier with all those road marches and runs up the Kolekole Pass. Apparently, the higher ups didn't think so. In the months leading up to the conversion, they added more physical training on Tuesday and Thursday evenings and we would form up as a company and march over to the PT field.

Typically, these extra PT sessions started out just like the morning sessions but they quickly shifted into an exercise regimen that would take us to complete muscle failure. I had to move from one exercise to another, not stopping until I was too weak to do any more. Then the formation would close ranks and we would run. The runs were for shorter distances than the morning runs but at a much faster pace.

PT wasn't over when the runs ended. Nope. Huffing and puffing, desperate to get air, we would remain in formation until most of us were breathing more normally. We would then be ordered to attention and put back in the extended formation for PT. More push-ups, more sit ups, on and on it went. Just when you knew you couldn't do any more, the torturous agony would end and the order "at ease" would be given.

I knew this wasn't the end though. Every one of these evening sessions ended with grass drills. Without a moment of reprieve, I'd see the whistle going to the PT leader's mouth and knew what that meant. Groaning, I somehow found the strength to get through this with the knowledge that it couldn't go on forever.

During this transition to light infantry, the morning PT sessions also evolved. More and more we would have rifle PT where we would incorporate the M16 rifle into the exercise program. I dreaded this form of PT. The rifle weighed about seven-and-a-half pounds' empty. Sounds light until you had to hold it in your outstretched arms, parallel to the ground for an eternity. The exercises were like our normal routines and done at a four count. Most of the calisthenics were performed with the rifle held at arm's length in front of me, to one side or the other, and above my head. Seven and a half pounds quickly turned into a ton and a half and made it impossible to continue the movements properly.

The worst was yet to come. Running with a rifle isn't as easy as it sounds. Strapping the rifle over the shoulder was the standard way it was carried but we didn't keep it there for the entire run. That would be too easy and therefore not an option for us. Nope, the "port arms" order would occasionally be given which required you to unsling it and hold it in front of you parallel to your body. To really spice things up, we would occasionally be ordered to run for short spells with the rifle held over our head. Yep, I hated rifle PT.

When I was processing out of the Army and preparing to return to civilian life, the division started dabbling in aerobics. That's right, aerobics! Someone, in their infinite wisdom, thought it would be good training for a light infantry unit to do aerobics. What was next, leg warmers and headbands? I am so glad I missed the aerobics phase of PT in the mornings.

Chapter 24
Homeward Bound

As my second enlistment ended, I was once again faced with a decision to make about my future and whether the army would be a part of it. This time it was my physical health that was the real deciding factor. All the physical demands of being in the infantry had taken a toll on me. I had sprained my right ankle countless times while in Hawaii. The prudent thing would have been to stay off the ankle the first time I sprained it until it healed. Same for the second time, third time, fourth and on and on. Prudence isn't exactly what happens when you're a grunt, especially a grunt in a leadership position.

I couldn't wimp out of physical activities because of a booboo. Commanders at every level frowned upon it and medics were cautious about exempting anyone from training unless something was broken. They worked for the same commanders that I did after all. Once I became a non-commissioned officer and placed in a leadership role, I had no choice but to keep running. I suffered in silence each time I sprained my ankle and ran through the pain. That's just how it was back then.

I don't even remember the very first time I sprained the ankle. I just know I didn't let it slow me down. You sprain your ankle marching, you keep marching. You sprain it running, you keep running. I never removed my footwear until we were done because the foot would swell up like a balloon and I would never get my boot back on.

And I sprained it again. And then again. And again…

I have no idea how many times it happened but eventually my ankle lost all stability and I would sprain it all the time, even just walking on a flat surface. To correct this, my ankle had to be reconstructed. I was sent to Tripler Army Medical Center for this procedure. Back then the procedure to correct ankle instability was to drill a hole through the ankle. A muscle from the right side of my foot was severed, fed through the hole, and secured on the other side. A very painful procedure that took months to recover from.

Being the hardcore idiot that I was, I only spent the first few days in bed following surgery before returning to duty. I was in a full cast and not allowed to put weight on it, but I refused to let it slow me down. I could still do my job of coordinating and scheduling training for the company if I used crutches and kept it elevated whenever I possible. I drove myself to and from work using my left leg to accelerate and brake and Marlon drove me everywhere I needed to go during the day. Looking back, I see this was stupid and not very safe.

I finally got the ankle rehabbed and returned to full duty. Unfortunately, all that running on a busted right ankle had caused me to overcompensate with my left leg and I was starting to have trouble with my left knee. In the infantry, it would be impossible to perform my job efficiently with knee and ankle problems. Plus, once I reenlisted at Fort Knox, I was placed in a career status and locked in to my primary MOS in the infantry. I am sure I could have gotten approval to change jobs for medical reasons if I pushed hard enough but I didn't believe I could maintain the high standards I had made for myself on bum legs.

There was one more factor that made my decision to leave the army easy. Every year, my mother and her friend Bob Reed, would come to the island to visit. Their first visit happened right after I won the Brigade NCO of the 3rd Quarter award. As luck would have it, their last visit was when I was contemplating my future. He had just built and opened a full-service hotel in Bedford, Indiana called the Stonehenge Lodge and was having management problems. I was completely unaware of this during their visit. Bob was very impressed with my military accomplishments and the conversations we had. He thought I would be a good solution for his hotel problems. Shortly after they got back home, my mom called and asked me if I would be interested in running the hotel for them when I was discharged.

Problem solved. I told my chain of command my decision and began the countdown towards the next phase of my life. I had one thing left on my list of goals and that was to receive a Meritorious Service Medal. I had discussed this with my company commander, Captain Young. He submitted the request for this award to the battalion commander on the basis that it was not only for everything that I had done for the unit, but for everything I had accomplished over my entire career.

The award was denied. Captain Young fought hard on my behalf but informed me the battalion commander wouldn't budge claiming he couldn't give this award to somebody who had missed so much PT the past year, even if I was recovering from ankle reconstruction. Never mind the fact that the surgery was necessary because I hadn't missed any PT the previous two years which resulted in me having to have the surgery in the first place. I was shocked to learn this, especially since I knew he had just given this award to his executive officer when he was reassigned after the year or so he served. This was a guy with the rank of a major who had less time in service, and a fraction of the duties and responsibilities that I had as company training NCO. As you can see, I am still bitter about this. I did receive my second Army Commendation Medal for my service. It is only fitting that the army never recorded this award into my military records. Not only did I not get the MSM I felt I had earned, but that final ACM that I was downgraded to isn't even included in my military file.

I was given an amazing opportunity to start a second career and I never looked back. I would re-enter the civilian world to be a hotel general manager. A year after I took this job, Mr. Reed bought another full-service hotel in Clarksville, Indiana. I was made general manager of it as well. I would successfully run both hotels for the next dozen or so years.

My time in the military instilled many strong leadership skills in me. I was blessed to work for some amazing people who taught me the importance of leading by setting a good example and taking care of your soldiers. Happy, well-trained soldiers required less supervision and did their jobs better. Treat them right and they will work hard for you. This is true in all aspects of life.

I was able to take all my knowledge and experience from the military and use it to be an effective leader in my new role as hotel manager.

Chapter 25
Closing

Like every person who has served in the military, I remain very proud of my military accomplishments and my status as a veteran. Cold War veterans may not have been able to serve during the war on terrorism but we played a key role in preparing the military for the successes it would have later.

The war in Vietnam and our final withdrawal had taken away a lot of credibility from the United States around the world. This paled in comparison to the chasm that it opened back home between the government and the public. An unpopular war from the beginning, the country's involvement caused a fervor of anti-war sentiment and protests that swept the entire nation. To the shame of many who protested, their misguided anger would be directed towards every veteran when they returned home. Brave men who had been drafted and answered their beloved country's call to arms would be ridiculed and humiliated in public.

The military would be tasked with the job of cleaning up its image and learning from the failures of Vietnam. One lesson learned was it had been too slow and bulky, geared towards large battles in open terrain where armored vehicles could operate. The confines of a jungle atmosphere limited the way we fought and showed as the need to change our strategies.

The Soviet Union had not been idle while we fought communism in Korea and Vietnam. While our defense budget was being spent on these wars, the Soviets and the Warsaw Pact were expanding their armies and growing their nuclear arsenal until they surpassed us in size and firepower. In the upcoming years, we would find ourselves in an arms race with them. Ronald Reagan would become president and change all of this.

President Reagan took office in January of 1981 and immediately made it clear that he thought communism was the biggest threat in the world and he wasn't going to be intimidated by it. We were on the brink of World War III and a full nuclear war for the first four or five years of his presidency, and my service. It was the veterans who served from the close of Vietnam through those critical years of Reagan's presidency who played a key part in its prevention with their vigilance and readiness.

I read about a meeting that took place years after the demise of the Soviet Union. A handful of the military leaders from the east and the west had gotten together to compare notes and discuss the respective doctrines in place for both sides. The part that caught my attention was the discussion of plans if war would have broken out. The use of nuclear weapons was included in every scenario the Warsaw Pact had in place. The significance of this was quite clear to me. The Fulda Gap that we were expected to defend in West Germany would have been ground zero.

Cold War veterans served while the military evolved from the slower heavy armor units to the more technologically advanced and faster vehicles in the eighties to light, rapidly deployable units that are utilized now. Our pain and sweat during this peacetime era was instrumental in the successful changes adopted by the military to face the current challenges in the war on terrorism. Just like the lessons learned from our failures in Vietnam, the military has learned from the struggles in Iraq and Afghanistan. We were integral in the transition to a lighter more mobile military, and today's soldiers will be instrumental in the evolution to combat these new terrorist threats into the future.

Cold War veterans were part of another significant change as the military became completely voluntary. The Selective Service Act was enacted in 1980 to change the way the draft could be used. It required all male citizens to register when they turned eighteen and they would remain eligible for service until they turned twenty-six. Since the Vietnam War, the military hasn't needed to utilize a draft to fill its ranks, finding people who were willing to step up of their own free will to protect this country and its interests around the world.

Peacetime is a relative term and for those serving in the armed forces there is no such thing as peacetime. There will always be threats in the world. As the only real super power left, the responsibility falls to us to support democracy and protect those who cannot protect themselves. For example, I wish we took a stronger stance against countries that are violent to their own people.

The soldiers who served during the time of the Cold War should not be ashamed because there was no war to fight. No veteran should ever be ashamed of his or her service. It takes a special person to voluntarily make a commitment to serve his or her country and, if called upon, die for it. We have a military like no other country because it is made up of soldiers who have volunteered to protect our freedoms. To soldiers, the United States is the greatest country in the world. Soldiers don't control the circumstances of when they serve so they prepare rigorously, always ready to answer that call without warning. There is no shame in this.

When I began dealing with my issues as a Cold War veteran living in a time of war, I realized most veterans from this era were dealing with this same turmoil. This led me to think about veterans who served during a period of declared war but were never in harm's way, serving in support or training roles away from combat. They were filling positions just as important and surely feel this same guilt when thanked for their service.

I wish I could say this book has resolved my feelings, but it hasn't. I still find myself trying to become one with the pew when the preacher asks veterans to stand and be recognized. I dread attending school programs on Veteran's Day and all the thanks that go with it.

I find myself mentioning this book as a conversation starter on this subject. I have found that few have ever considered this dilemma, yet everyone seems to know of someone who falls into this category. Hearing me talk about how I felt makes them realize their friend or relative is dealing with this as well. So, my crusade continues and I hope my story helps people become more aware of what some veterans go through. More importantly, I want other Cold War veterans to know they are not alone if they are struggling with this.

People's misconceptions about how it feels being a peacetime veteran is understandable. The real travesty is that most states make a strong distinction in their benefits for veterans, particularly disabled veterans. State benefits are in place for disabled veterans if their service occurred during a time of declared war by Congress. In my case, I have a disability rating now of eighty percent with more than half of my disabilities involving my legs. Since I didn't serve during a time of war, most of the benefits of the State of Indiana are unavailable to me. Veterans should be able to expect the best treatment for their disabilities for the rest of their lives and there should be no distinction between war and peacetime veterans who were injured while serving. A military disability is still a military disability no matter when it occurred during a career of service.

One disclaimer; I tried to be as accurate as I could, but please keep in mind I went through all of this almost thirty years ago. This project brought back many memories of all the great guys I was honored to serve with. I wish I could have mentioned them all.

This was a trying time in our history and most people have no idea what it was like for those of us who served in the military during it all. I tried to give you a sprinkle of this history throughout this book, but let me apologize now to any history buffs - I wasn't a history major. I wrote this from my perspective as best I could.

I am extremely proud of my service and feel honored and privileged to hold the title "Cold War Veteran." During the process of publishing this book, I have connected with hundreds of other veterans who served during this unofficial "war." I have been moved beyond words from the gratitude and thanks given to me for writing about what it was like serving during the Cold War. The overwhelming support from veterans has convinced me there needs to be more said on this subject. I have started writing the sequel. Each chapter in the follow-up will feature the story of different veterans, different jobs, during different years.

Thank you for taking the time to read my story.

"I Can Do All Things Through Christ Who Strengthens Me" – Philippians 4:13

ABOUT THE AUTHOR

Resides in Bedford, Indiana with his wife Marsha and their three granddaughters; Sage, Jade, and Harmonie. Father to five children; Natalie, Bambie, Amber, Bob Jr, and Rob.

Served in the United States Army from November 1980 to March 1988. Worked as general manager of two full service hotels from 1988 to 2001. During this period, he founded and served ten years on the Lawrence County tourism commission.

www.weweresoldierstoo.com